RECOVERING FROM RECOVERY

One gay man's journey toward sexual and emotional freedom during and after sobriety

Adam Fitzgerald

KDP ISBN: 9798399066820
eBook ASIN: B0C8G5KBKM

First paperback edition August 2023
Edited by Ellen Vessels
Cover art by Denis Trauchessec

Printed by Kindle Direct Publishing in the USA
kdp.amazon.com

Disclaimer
The material in this publication is of the nature of general
comment only, and does not represent professional advice. It
is not intended to provide specific guidance for particular
circumstances and it should not be relied on as the basis for
any decision to take action or not take action on any matter
which it covers. Readers should obtain professional advice
where appropriate, before making any such decision. To the
maximum extent permitted by law, the author and publisher
disclaim all responsibility and liability to any person, arising
directly or indirectly from any person taking or not taking
action based on the information in this publication.

For Robbie, who never got the help he needed.

INTRODUCTION

We will never be without pain. Anyone who has suffered, to any degree, knows they will never be completely free of that experience. The idea of being unharmed and unhurt, though beautiful, is an impossible goal. Time may heal all wounds, but scars remain. There is, however, great power and joy in the reduction of harm, particularly in minimizing the harm we inflict upon ourselves.

We seem to have an obsession with an "all-or-nothing" way of thinking, especially in the United States. Winner takes all. Go big or go home. While many a capitalist or politician has reached great career heights driven by this mentality, when it comes to inner healing, this ideal is highly problematic. Self-love will not always be at 100 percent, and that does not indicate failure. It is a journey with ups and downs to know and enact kindness toward oneself.

The night of April 5, 2009, I went on yet another drunken bender and woke up the next day in a stranger's bed, once again not knowing where I was. I grabbed my phone to find several missed calls from a friend who needed help moving. He was sober, so when I finally pulled myself together and made my way to his place, I spent the next several hours trying

5

to avoid getting too close to him so he would not smell my alcohol-soaked breath. I was there to help him, but even so, I was drowning in shame.

I walked into an Alcoholics Anonymous (AA) meeting later that day feeling broken and very sad. I had been to several meetings before, wanting to get my drinking under control without abstaining completely. This time I came in with the idea that it needed to stop. I needed to stop drinking.

At the time, I believed I needed to quit drinking completely, largely because no other options were presented to me. In hindsight, I do not know if that was true, but it was my journey. I do not regret taking that step. What I do regret, or rather, what I am now learning to dismantle, is the all-or-nothing mentality applied to my drinking and to the rest of my subsequent healing and growth.

When we talk about recovery from substance abuse, we speak only in extremes. A person is either 100 percent substance free, or they have slipped and failed. Complete abstinence is the only celebrated and therefore the only acceptable measure of success. The word we use to describe taking even one drink is "relapse," defined by Oxford Languages as "a deterioration of one's health after a period of improvement."

If a formerly daily-drinker now has one night or a weekend of drinking every so often, that person is told they have relapsed and must start counting again from zero. We do not celebrate that person for taking much better care of themselves, for drinking much less than before. Less is not good enough. Instead we tell them they have failed and must start over. Try again, and maybe you will succeed this time. Start counting again at day one.

Where is the love in that?

This all-or-nothing mentality regarding those struggling with drugs and/or alcohol cannot possibly be the only—and certainly not universally the best—method for everyone. While it may have worked for me at the time, for a time, it also caused me harm. To this day, when it comes to my mental health, I can still view anything short of perfection as a failure. A slip. A relapse. I absorbed this pass/fail mentality, and now when I have a bad day or an irrational reaction to a trigger, my first thought is often, "See. I am no better than before. I am still a mess."

This harmful and extreme way of evaluation is certainly not unique to the world of substance abuse recovery, but it is the application in that world that I want to address. This success-or-failure mentality may have kick-started my recovery, but it arrested my healing. This book focuses on my sexuality, not only because sex is a tangible indicator of deeper issues, but also because my pursuit of an active sex life is what caused me to question and move beyond AA. Sex was the catalyst that allowed me to begin to examine the underlying mentality of my alcohol recovery.

Learning to accept my sexuality, my promiscuity, and my unorthodox desires was and is at the core of learning to accept myself. I speak to you from somewhere along this journey, not at its end. I tell the stories of my sex life not to shock or because I think you'll be impressed, but to be open and honest about sex and to shed sex-negativity. Embracing the word "slut" (a person who loves to give and receive pleasure from as many people as possible) has opened me up to an entirely new way of thinking.

I do not seek to rewrite or dismantle Alcoholics Anonymous. "The program," as it is often called, is something I once participated in, but no longer do. This is my own journey from a newly sober man who was terrified of substance-free sex to a sex-positive, joyous, and liberated slut who now drinks in moderation. The words I write are my own, and I do not claim that my experiences in AA are a universal truth. I am aware that this qualifier will not stop some people from being very angry with what I have to say. I am okay with that. I think.

For more than twelve years, I did not consume an alcoholic beverage or a narcotic. Today, I am no longer sober. I'm also not sure I believe in the concept of alcoholism as a "disease," at least not in the incurable sense. I certainly do not believe in broadly and universally applying the diagnosis to anyone who struggles with substance abuse.

On the question of the "disease," it is important to note that I am neither a doctor nor a scientist, so I have no expertise on the medical aspects of alcohol abuse. The American Psychiatric Association recognizes "alcoholism" as the equivalent of "alcohol dependence." The American Hospital Association, the American Public Health Association, the National Association of Social Workers, and the American College of Physicians all classify alcoholism as a disease. According to the National Center for Biotechnology Information, there are genetic components that can affect how a person processes alcohol, but according to the National Library of Medicine,

"it should be emphasized that while genetic differences affect risk, there is no 'gene for alcoholism,' and both environmental and

social factors weigh heavily on the outcome. Genetic factors affect the risk not only for alcohol dependence, but also the level of alcohol consumption and the risk for alcohol-associated diseases, including cirrhosis and upper GI cancers. Knowing that genetic factors affect risk does not mean that we know which specific variants contribute, nor how."

(https://www.ncbi.nlm.nih.gov/pmc/articles/PMC4056340/)

All this to say that the research on the genetics of alcoholism is ongoing, but science has not yet found a specific cause. Generally, it is thought that the source of the disease can be genetic, environmental, or both. There is not one factor or cause, but most importantly there is no method of diagnosis. The alcoholic or addict self-diagnoses, often by raising their hand in a twelve-step meeting. There is no known cure. Nor is there scientific proof that a drinking or drug problem is a permanent state, even though this assumption is widely accepted. We simply do not know if that is true.

I decided to largely drop the rhetoric of "alcoholic" and "addict" as I wrote this text, instead referring to a person as struggling with substance abuse. The use of the label "addict" implies that substance abuse is an ingrained weakness or inherent fault that cannot be cured but must be dealt with. Such an implication glosses over the source or reason behind a person's substance abuse and the pain and trauma experienced, instead focusing on the reaction. We pity the resulting coping mechanism rather than admire the strength of the survivor.

In labeling a person an addict or alcoholic, there is a nearly universal agreement that anything other than a zero-use life is a failure. I have come to believe that not only have we set inordinate standards of achievement, but we have also placed the emphasis on the consumption (or not) of the drug of choice rather than on the reasons a person is abusing that drug in the first place. Rather than on healing.

I also reject any notion that one solution fits all individuals, no matter their story. I am wary, in particular, if that singular method of supposed healing only offers a black-and-white, success-or-failure system of evaluation. Life is a journey, not a pass/fail exam. There cannot be a singular, universally applicable measure of movement toward a better life and a better self.

I drank in excess in order to avoid some very specific things, and it was not until stepping away from AA and into therapy that I discovered that truth. Growing up, I developed a sense that I was only lovable if I was useful. In a somewhat chaotic household, I often witnessed and was occasionally the victim of violence from my father. The most sensitive and emotional of my siblings, I became a source of emotional support for my mother at an age when I was entirely too young. I was also a young homosexual in rural America in the '70s and '80s, and society's feelings about homosexuality were all too clear. As such, I developed two terribly damaging inner truths.

The first is a belief that I need to control and manage chaos wherever it exists in my life. I choose career paths that frequently put me "in charge," often of people and situations that are unstable. My relationships have been almost entirely with charming, exciting men with substance abuse problems. I hurl myself toward instability, needing desperately to be the fixer, the saver, and the source of calm and love. Unfortunately, I tie my self-worth to the success of that management. Life is messy, and I choose messier than most. When I could not manage the mayhem, (which I considered my entire and sole responsibility), I perceived myself to be a useless failure, and so I got drunk.

The second belief, one I still struggle with, is that I am not inherently lovable. I am only worthy of love if I am useful, and consequently the moment that I fail or cease to be useful, you will stop loving me. I believe that everyone I encounter, from coworkers to friends to lovers, deserves love simply on the basis of their human existence. I, however, do not. I needed to earn the love that the rest of you already deserved just by being alive, and so I got drunk.

The program of Alcoholics Anonymous helped at first, but quickly became an obstacle to my growth. I was so in need of approval, so desperate to do the program well, that I even changed the narrative of my own life to fit the ideal twelve-step success story. I transferred the mentality of my alcohol abuse over to my recovery and perceived my own life in a way that I thought would be most well received and then shared that story. I believed wholeheartedly in the notion of an incurable disease because it provided me with another, new excuse not to address the sources of my pain.

In therapy, I was finally able to uncover and admit these things and begin the process of harm reduction. A few years in, I still have a long way to go, but I am healing. One of the revelations I had in those sessions was learning that I used AA the same way I used alcohol, swapping one for the other. My story, as I told it to my fellows, minimized all the damage of my childhood and other abusive relationships. I instead heaped all of the blame onto my poor choices, my failures, and my drinking. Rather than reach out for love and acceptance because my pain and my past had caused my excessive drinking, I reversed the order and declared that my drinking had caused all of my problems. In that scenario, I could be both the villain and the hero of my own tale, but never the victim.

Healing is ongoing and never complete, so even after my thinking began to change, I chose to continue therapy for several years without drinking. My therapist and I spent more than two years discussing the possibility and creating a plan before I drank again. During that work, I began to understand that my drinking problem was a reaction to my past and not an incurable condition. Now, as a person who consumes alcohol in moderation, I seek a life of sexual and emotional freedom and no longer desire a path of lifelong sobriety.

It may seem odd that I, a man who went without a drink for twelve-plus years, should state that I do not believe in abstinence as the best solution. Over time and with experience, my ideas have changed as I have evolved. It began when I no longer believed that a 2:00 a.m. orgy with people in various states of intoxication was a threat to sobriety, because I had been there, sober, many times. In time, I also stopped being ashamed of saying I went to an orgy, which is a beautiful, group experience of consensual, shared ecstasy.

I am continually healing, learning, and growing. I sometimes stumble backwards, falling into old habits and acting out of deeply ingrained, childish fears. I have more questions than answers, and it is likely I may write things today that I will no longer believe, or will believe differently, in the future. I stopped drinking several years ago because I had a severe drinking problem. Today, I know that the issues I needed to address were deeper, more complicated, and began much, much earlier than my first drink.

SEX and SOBRIETY

In early sobriety, I began to unpack my association of sex with substances. Throughout my adult life up to the point when I quit drinking, my sexual endeavors had largely occurred only when there were alcohol or drugs in my system. From the time I left my parents' home in 1994 until I stopped drinking fifteen years later, I drank nearly every night. I was not frequently a day-drinker, so there were certainly sexual experiences with my then-boyfriends that happened sober during the daytime. But sex usually happened in the evening, especially with strangers or new partners, so prior to 2009, the vast majority of my sex life involved alcohol and sometimes drugs.

Born in 1976, I grew up in rural New England in the era of the AIDS crisis. I was just young enough to not yet be sexually active during the height of the crisis, but I was old enough to absorb the shock, shame, guilt, and fear, not to mention the nationalized, escalated hatred of gay men. I was a teenager, knowing I was gay but not yet admitting it, and everything I heard about sex was that gay sex would kill me and that I probably deserved it. In my twenties and early thirties, I woke up in a panic if I had had sex the night before, sure that I would become sick and possibly die.

As a newly sober man, I was therefore terrified of sex. Without that liquid courage to calm my fears and insecurities, I had no idea how to have sex. The mayhem inside my head ranged from thinking I might burst into tears as soon as someone kissed me to being sure I would prematurely ejaculate the second an attractive man touched my penis. I genuinely thought that without alcohol I would either cry, orgasm immediately, or both. It was not a sexy image.

Before getting sober, I loved the first time with a new partner, that labyrinth of discovering a new body, finding out what turned him on, and wordlessly allowing him to explore the same on me. I do not want monogamy for many reasons, but a major one is that I am not willing to relinquish the joy of that newness. But suddenly, that joy and discovery I craved now felt scary, vulnerable, and impossible. I did not know how to have sex without alcohol to help me escape the shame that told me I was ugly and unlovable.

But I needed sex then. I need sex now. Sex is an expression of who I am. Sex is beautiful and fun, defying logic and allowing me to step outside the whirring, intellectual, and ongoing analysis inside my head. Sex allows me to understand others on a physical, wordless, and intimate level. It has been a part of my identity throughout my entire adult life. Sex is awesome.

Six months into sobriety, I had not had sex even once. I was scared and confused, not knowing how to separate my sexual desires from the alcohol and drugs that had accompanied most of my sexual experiences. If sex had always involved substances, were they intrinsically linked? And if so, was having sex akin to getting drunk?

I finally said yes to an advance, and John (I will use pseudonyms throughout) was on his way to my apartment. I was so scared. He fascinated me, this fellow sober man who told me openly and unashamedly, "I want us to fuck." He did not want to go on a date and he did not think we were falling in love. He (also less than a year sober) just wanted to have sex with me. Sober sex.

The day of our planned encounter, I was spinning with panic. I am so grateful my roommates were not home that day to witness me pacing the apartment, probably looking insane. As I waited during the hour between his "On my way!" text and the ringing of my buzzer, I contemplated canceling at least a dozen times. By the time he arrived, I was fully terrified. I was sure it was all going to go horribly wrong and he would leave disappointed.

It turns out the sex was really good. It was more than a decade ago, so I do not remember all of the details, but I do remember that we flipped, we licked and sucked every part of each other's bodies, and we made each other orgasm, hard. Happily, I neither cried nor pre-ejaculated.

I also remember *not* having to check the floor to see if we had used condoms as I had done so many mornings after blackout sex (this was before PrEP). I remember not struggling for his name, not wondering what neighborhood I was in, and not regretting anything. Sober, honest, and wildly horny, John and I fucked, and it was fun.

A few weeks later, after having sex several more times, John suddenly changed the way he interacted with me. He became evasive, canceled plans last minute, and was vague about his reasons. I was confused; he was a fuck-buddy, and suddenly he was acting like our relationship was something else, so I confronted him. He told me he did not want to be my boyfriend. "Oh," I replied, "I don't want to be your boyfriend either. We would be a terrible couple!" He laughed, we hugged, and we are friends to this day.

I learned important things from John. I began to have an inkling that my love of casual sex was not a part of my drinking problem. It is a part of my identity and not a problem at all. Because I had been drunk for almost every casual sexual encounter in my past, I had mentally attached a coincidental negativity and shame to uncoupled sex. It turns out I just really like having sex.

I also tested the waters of being honest and open about my sexuality. John and I had a simple conversation about both our desires and perceptions of the other, and nothing imploded. When I said to him that I didn't want to couple, I just blurted out a reaction without thinking, but it was the truth. I was able to say, "I don't want to be with you. I just like fucking you." No guilt. No hiding. After years of being ashamed of my desire for casual sex, the mental shift was enormous.

In the rooms of AA, however, new relationships were highly discouraged during the first year, when sobriety would be the most fragile. Sex was sometimes more of a grey area, but I would often hear gay men preach the dangers of casual sex and the "slippery slope" of gay sex apps and make sweeping declarations of how casual sex was never satisfying and only a "product of our disease." I became alternately frustrated and ashamed. As I was discovering that maybe my sexuality had not been a product of my using, but rather something my using allowed me to express, I was regularly hearing that if

I had casual sex, I would be drunk in a matter of minutes. I was also hearing that casual sex was invalid, cheap, and lesser.

My sponsor, an amazing and beautiful man, would just chuckle. "Take what you want and leave the rest," he would say, one of the few AA idioms he adopted into his own vernacular. He would tell me to breathe and that not everything I heard had to apply to me. When I was particularly riled up and struggling with a slut-shaming rant from one of the fellows, he would just say, "AA is not a hotbed for mental health. Sometimes you should just ignore someone."

He was so calm. Over and over in AA I would hear that if I did not follow the path and take all the advice of "elders" I would end up drunk, miserable, and alone. From my sponsor, I would hear to breathe, smile, and use only what was useful. At the end of the day, if I went to bed not-drunk, I was doing everything right. His kindness gave me the freedom to question, and in that questioning, I started to discover some things about my own fear and shame and how easily I could absorb that from others.

People often say that AA is a cult, an accusation that offends many of its members. I, too, disagree with that assertion for the simple reason that a cult has a leader. AA has its founders and its text, like many a religion, but there is no living figurehead. The knowledge and thought that comes out of the rooms of AA is a collective consciousness formed by a group of people with a relatable experience.

There are, however, some pretty cultish elements. You will often hear people say, smacking of worship mentality, "it says right there in The Big Book" (the colloquialism for the book *Alcoholics Anonymous*) as if quoting a divine text. Many more than imply that they've been "saved" by AA or have seen a proverbial light, metaphors regularly employed in cults or religious extremism. The most cultish, perhaps, is a passage read at the beginning of most meetings: "Those who do not recover are people who cannot or will not completely give themselves to this simple program, usually men and women who are constitutionally incapable of being honest with themselves."

There is nothing wrong with celebrating a group, book, or way of thinking that has improved your life; that is, until the members of that group believe that theirs is the best way, the only way, and the path for all. There is a fine line between accepting the wisdom of those with experience and losing one's identity to a collective (and thereby adopting a false sense of superiority over those outside of it). I find that line to be crossed all too often within the rooms of recovery.

There are certainly benefits to collective wisdom and strength in being part of a community of people who have overcome the same obstacle. With every moment of "I can't do this" came the support of hundreds of people who said, "Yes, you can!" with an assuredness that comes only from having done so themselves. I took strength and comfort from my AA friends, many of whom are still in my life today.

But there is also inherent danger in a leaderless organization powered by groupthink. There are no psychological experts, addiction specialists, or fact-checkers of any kind to hold that group mentality accountable. An elder can make an assertion that quickly becomes accepted as an inherent truth. That person's long-term sobriety gives them an authority which, you, newly sober, are afraid to question. The primary example is the group's diagnosis of every member as having an incurable disease, with no expertise to make such diagnoses.

After many years of attempting and failing to control my drinking, I was scared to question the methods of anyone who had achieved sobriety. I was messy, a bit lost, and extremely disappointed in myself. I would sit there wide-eyed, listening to these men and women who had vanquished a problem which I had failed to conquer, so I took in anything and everything they told me. I wanted desperately to follow their path. In the beginning, I blindly followed any advice I was given. I certainly did not want to be labeled as "constitutionally incapable" of honesty or of following simple instructions.

Some of what I learned early on in AA is valuable and still applicable to my life today. Make your bed in the morning, they told me, and so I did. When I returned home at night, there in front of me was the evidence that I had woken up sober enough to make my bed, which helped me to stay sober again that night. Many years later, I still make my bed every morning, and it always feels good when I come home.

The problem was that all advice could seem like good advice. I thought that if I failed to incorporate any guidance proclaimed by someone "with time" (long term sobriety), I would end up drunk. I would sit in these rooms absorbing beautiful, healing power, surrounded by people who had stopped chemically harming themselves. That energy would often override the nagging doubt when I heard something that made me hesitate, especially those broad declarations of how one must or must not be, act, do, or think, especially about sex.

Yet I did (and to a degree still do) believe that some principles of AA work and lead to a better life. With the help of my sponsor, who had no problem rejecting anything that did not sit right with him, I began to reconfigure this guidance into a format that worked for me, beginning with eliminating the overly religious aspects written by cis, white, Christian, straight men of a certain set of values that largely do not apply to my life. Bill, Bob, and I do not have the same idea of what constitutes a good life.

Newly sober, I felt alive, healed, strong, and even wise. As I began to mentally edit the text and filter the advice, there was a little voice that kept asking more questions and raising doubts about the universality of what I was being told. It may have started the first time I read the wildly sexist chapter entitled "To Wives" that is still in the latest edition of the book, containing guidelines for how to be the best wife to your now-sober husband. It reads like a checklist from a 1940s ladies' magazine.

I began to wonder if some of what I was hearing in AA was all a bit too dogmatic (and old-school, hetero, and Christian), if this advice and guidance was coming from people who were living as I wanted to live. Does being sober give someone the authority to tell me how to be or act, sexually or otherwise?

Was I actually addressing my problem or just indulging in a temporary solution because it felt so much better? Do I really have an incurable disease, or did I just use alcohol to cope with my feelings and fears?

I believe we crave intimacy. We desire connection. We want love. Sex, sober or not, can be an expression of that, a physical and intimate connection between two (or more) people. It is a particularly American conundrum that we celebrate sex and sexuality everywhere in the media, yet continue to have extreme shame and puritanical ideals surrounding sexuality in our personal interactions.

My slow retreat from AA led me to therapy, which prompted me to ask the bigger questions and begin to unpack my hidden past. Throughout this process I dug into the question "Why did I drink so much?" As my life became more like what I desired it to be, as my sexuality became more liberated and truthful, and as I addressed my deeply ingrained fear of love and intimacy, I discovered, more so with each session, that my problematic drinking was the result of and not the cause of my trauma, fear, and connections between dependency and love I learned early in life. Having deeply explored and expanded my sexuality without chemical enhancement, I could then see that the majority of my past sexual exploits were not shameful mistakes, but true desires unleashed by inebriation. I can now have sex with or without alcohol, and happily so in either case.

So, after a bit of time in AA, and having gone through the twelve steps, I needed to return to what I had learned and weed out what did and did not apply to me. Rather than throw out everything that had worked, I began to rethink those guidelines found in the steps, keeping what could help in my present journey. Below are the leftovers of what I have kept (and rewritten), broken into twelve parts.

These are not an attempt to create new steps or a new program. They are an ever-changing reflection on my own past and my present, ongoing learning. The twelve chapters that follow often focus on sexuality and sexual healing because sex opened my mind to question everything else. Sex is also a part of my identity and life. I cannot apply any "steps" to my life without considering sex. Or, more accurately, I don't want to.

1. Learning where I am powerless and where I am not

I seek to regain my power both from my past and in the embrace of my present sexuality.

AA Step One as I learned it: We admitted we were powerless over alcohol and that our lives had become unmanageable.

When we feel powerless, we seek out power. So many drunks and drug abusers come into recovery programs wrecked, sad, and lonely. Our relationships were in trouble or destroyed; we can't see over the pile of lies we have told to cover up our using; and we need help. In AA, I and many others found that help.

But did quitting drinking give me any actual, useful knowledge on how to be a better person in the world? Did I regain any of my power?

With anything that improves our outlook and our life, we feel more empowered. Having journeyed so far from lost to found, from messy to stable, from miserable to something approaching happiness, we believe that we have found *the* secret. We see only the great distance traveled, which can easily give us a false sense of accomplishment, but our perspective is limited.

Having come from the depths of abusing alcohol seven days a week, stumbling through most days hungover and ashamed, sobriety seemed like a gigantic leap forward. But all I did was quit drinking. I simply returned my life to point zero, putting it back at the same level as everyone else who isn't living in a chemically induced haze.

It turns out, I do not know better than anyone else how to live or be. Honestly, I can be kind of a mess. Ask any of my exes what it is like to live with my chaotic mind and clumsy nature. I forget not to curse when children are around, I am terrible at going to bed on time, and I break a glass or a plate about once a week. I cannot count the number of times I have said, "Yeah, I probably should have kept that opinion to myself."

But at the time, I believed I had accomplished much more than quitting drinking. I was under the false impression that a secret had been revealed to me, that I had unlocked a wealth of knowledge on how to live. In my mind, I had boarded a great ship, sailing through the world with this newfound knowledge. More accurately, I had acquired a pair of arm floaties like those a child uses to stay afloat in the pool.

We see this delusion in religious extremism, with people thinking they have found "the light" and the only answers to all of life's eternal questions. We see it in those with success and wealth thinking they are now experts on all aspects of life. We see it in whiteness, with have-mores thinking that we know more when instead we've just been handed more. And we see this in recovery, where so many of us changed from disasters to functioning members of society, so we think we know how life really works and therefore what everyone else should be doing.

The humbling truth is that each of us is only a somewhat-expert on that small slice of life between where we were and where we are now. I may be of use to a person trying to reduce their drinking or drug use because I had experiences I can share and a relatable point of view. I do not, however, know how to fix any of life's problems, and I still have plenty of my own. I made a positive change in my life, but the enormity of that change led me to believe I had expertise where I had none.

To look at this simply, I do not go to a yoga teacher for advice on my taxes. I go to an accountant. When that friend who labels their love life a "disaster" gives me dating advice, I nod, smile, and promptly ignore them. Elsewhere, outside of AA, I take advice from only those people who are closer than I am to success in the topic at hand, and not from people with no knowledge or experience. I heard a lot of declarative opinions in AA about what was and was not "sober behavior," particularly in regard to sex. But why would I believe that someone having little or no sex would also have knowledge on how to have a healthy, active, and fulfilling sex life?

As such, I had to stop listening to a lot of gay men in AA when it came to sex. Men with nonexistent sex lives, declaring a condemnation (and often a terror) of casual sex, did not have a life I aspired to. I struggled to separate good and bad advice for one simple reason: fear. Each time I thought, "I don't want to live like that person," I also feared that my desires might be the voice of my sickness, and the response, "That's your disease talking!" was one I regularly heard in those rooms.

When I had those doubts, there were all too many members of AA ready and willing to confirm them, probably fueled by their own fear and shame. I was discovering that what I wanted was a life of sexual freedom and positivity wherein I would have multiple partners and open myself up to a wider range of sexual experiences. So why would I absorb their shame?

I have no problem with monogamy. If it makes you and your partner happy, I love that for you and I want you to enjoy everything about it. I also want you to show the same respect and kindness to me for choosing another lifestyle. We do not need to condemn or condone anyone else's sexual choices. We could just let another's happiness determine our response.

I remember distinctly the day one of my exes and I broke up, sitting on his couch. He was a monogamous person, and he knew from the start that I was not. We had tried so many compromises, but each left both of us feeling unsatisfied and untrue to ourselves. We sat on that couch and cried a little and hugged a lot, knowing we had both genuinely made an effort for the other. We also both knew it could not work. Instead of resenting each other and continuing in a relationship where neither was happy, we let each other go, hoping the other would find what they were looking for.

The gift that he gave me was to reconsider how strictly I had defined myself. While he and I were too far apart in our beliefs and desires to find a workable middle ground, he did challenge me to examine what was true and what was just something I had decided. Proudly non-monogamous, had I let the pendulum swing too far? He reminded me that though I do not want anything resembling a monogamous life, there is pleasure and joy on his end of the spectrum as well. I am grateful to him for teaching me that I do not need to limit myself. I hope I gave the same to him.

We all have a wide spectrum of desires and sexuality, yet we feel an overwhelming need to place ourselves at a singular point on the scale and to label the rest of the scale as "not me" and often as "not good." This is inauthentic at best and self-loathing at worst. Today, I am an active, proud slut. I also love partnered sex, waking up and cuddling with my boyfriend, feeling his love and affection. I do not need to condemn my romantic side to embrace my slutty side, or vice versa.

To be blunt, I may want to suck dick fairly often, but I also love making dinner, watching a movie, a one-on-one romantic night with my boyfriend (if I have one). All of these parts of me are real and they do not negate each other. I, like all humans, am capable of multiple desires even if they are seemingly in conflict. That conflict leads us to decide and categorize certain parts of ourselves as good and others as bad, childish, or false. We also categorize others as good or bad, and in doing so we limit each other's potential and deny the fullness and richness of our humanity.

Why can't we celebrate the entire spectrum of human experience and sexuality and relish in the interconnectedness of our desires? Why can't we support another's choices, even when they do not match our own? This inauthentic need to choose which parts of ourselves and others are right, good, or true is part of what pushes me away from monogamy.

An example, having nothing to do with sex, is the life of one of my older brothers. He lives next door to my mother in the small town where we grew up. He has a wife, two children, a mortgage, and an enormous lawn. He works in the high school we both attended. He loves his life.

My brother's life would be my own personal inferno. I could not imagine moving back home and working in my old high school, then coming home to a wife and two kids. Last time I visited, he invited me to go snowshoeing at dawn. Snowshoeing. At DAWN. Every detail of his daily existence and every major life choice he has made are the exact opposite of what I want, yet I am overjoyed for him and extremely proud of him. I am thrilled that this person I love is living his best life. My brother does not really understand non-monogamy, but he doesn't care, unlike many others. He does not judge my life either, and he just wants me to be happy. But no, I did not go snowshoeing.

I wonder if the reason so many people are against a non-monogamous lifestyle is less because they are afraid that their partner might want it and more because they're scared that they secretly desire it themselves. I do not believe that my choices are better for anyone other than myself. I do believe that it is dishonest to pretend that one stops having desires for anyone else the moment they "fall in love." I also believe that sex with a stranger (or multiple strangers) is not the opposite of love. It is not the antithesis of intimacy. Sex with a stranger is not inherently without connection, because the antithesis to intimacy is not brevity.

Where and why did we learn that casual sex is inherently disconnected? The implication is that two strangers cannot possibly be intimate, whereas a committed couple has, automatically, a greater level of intimacy. Anybody who has been both in a relationship and had multiple sexual partners knows this notion is not universally true. I have had many beautiful, intense sessions where I made love to another man I knew only for a few hours, and we explored and shared each other's bodies in a way that was deeply, soul-fulfillingly intimate. I have also had mediocre, disconnected, mechanical sex with long-term partners. Intimacy is a choice between partners, not a given set of external parameters determined by time.

A few years ago, I went to a gym/sauna in Paris. The upper floor is a sports facility, and downstairs is a winding maze of corridors, slings, and private rooms for sex. I had been there for about an hour and had mediocre sex with two men. The second was perhaps high on some substance and I disengaged from him fairly quickly. I was thinking the afternoon had been a bust and was about to leave, when a beautiful man, mustached and tall and sexy, caught my eye. He nodded toward a room, and in we went.

We had really good sex. It was hard, quick, dirty, sweaty, solidly enjoyable and deeply visceral. We kissed, sucked, and fucked, and we both orgasmed loudly and wonderfully, collapsing onto the mat together. He leaned over and kissed me and then lay down beside me.

For the next thirty or forty minutes, we held each other and did not speak. His hands traced every part of my body, and his lips kissed me, all over, lightly and softly. I traced the lines of his face with one finger and stroked his hair. Several times we kissed, slowly and so softly that there was sometimes more air than contact between our lips. More than once we pulled one another close, connecting with what I can only say was love. He or I would occasionally drift in and out of sleep, but never let go of the physical connection and spiritual consciousness of the other.

We felt at the same time when the moment was over. He kissed me one last time and said, "*Merci.*" He walked out the door, and I stayed for a few more minutes, basking in the beauty of what had just happened. I saw him later in the locker room as he was getting dressed, but we exchanged only a smile. He left before me and I have never seen him again.

When I recounted the story to a friend she cried out, almost frantically, "Why didn't you get his number?!" I was baffled, wondering what story she had just heard. "Because," I replied gently, "it was already perfect. Beginning, middle, and end." She actually began to cry, confused and unable to accept that I could let go of what could have been, in her version, potential for love. In my version, it was already love. I did not miss out on anything. That man and I exchanged a flawless gift.

If we predetermine the parameters of what can and cannot be an intimate experience, we preemptively negate incredible possibilities. Intimacy can exist and thrive in so many different ways. My first boyfriend, who let me feel and express love for the first time, shared intimacy with me. So did the man who first choked me during sex as he carefully asked with his hands how hard, how tight, and how long he could do so. That first boyfriend will be in my life forever, and that other man could walk by me on the street and I would not recognize him. Both are beautiful. Both are right. Both were intimate. Both are valid.

Yet even as these beautiful experiences accumulate in my life, I can still stumble into doubt and question their validity. I can still hear those voices from when I first got sober that told me I should not have been in that sauna at all. The anti-sex and anti-gay messages of my youth still haunt me. Particularly for men my age or older, the residual terror of HIV and AIDS instilled in us in the '80s and '90s is palpably vibrating underneath our words and experiences. And I still feel the pressure of a society that tells me that what I experienced was not love if it was not coupled.

What I now know is that alcohol did not make me fearful or powerless. I excessively consumed alcohol because I had become this way, and the booze quieted my whirling mind, my raging fear, and my debilitating belief that I do not deserve to be loved or enjoy sex. I lost control of parts of my life to excessive consumption of alcohol, but quitting drinking did not restore my self-worth. It was only a first step.

In AA meetings, you will often hear that the first step, admitting you are powerless over alcohol, is the only step you have to do perfectly. At first, I believed what I was taught, that alcohol took my power away. In fact, it was already gone long before I began drinking. A society that hated my sexual orientation, a violent past, and countless other experiences left me a powerless child, afraid of owning my own space. The AIDS crisis and American media telling me there was a gay cancer that many believed god had sent to punish the homos took my power away.

Later, I sacrificed more of my power to a society that told me I needed to "grow up," "settle down," and conform to a life with only one partner. I drank in response to these feelings of powerlessness, and then I handed that power over to AA and sober men and women. Many years before that first drunken experience, I had sacrificed my power, so with alcohol (and then AA) I simply changed who I perceived was holding the power I had lost as a child.

Many members of AA will dispute me on this point, but I simply do not believe all problematic consumption should be labeled as alcoholism or drug addiction, nor as a permanent condition. The use of "admitting" and "powerless" implies not only a universally unsolvable problem (an incurable disease), but one that existed before the trauma, shame, abuse, and self-loathing that causes people to veer toward excessive consumption in the first place. My abuse of alcohol was a product of my past, not something I was born with and certainly not the cause of my problems.

As a young man, I never directly addressed these sources of pain and fear. I developed a pattern of ignoring my inner voices throughout the day and then drinking them quiet every night. But ignoring my demons did not diminish them. I continually needed more and more alcohol and/or drugs to keep their voices at bay. Eventually, even that failed as my psyche learned to push through my drunkenness. By the end of that period of heavy drinking, the self-loathing was there no matter how much I consumed.

I needed to admit to the abuse of my substance of choice in order to begin to heal. I needed to quiet that chaos in order to look at deeper issues. There was a calming effect and a newfound strength in finally saying, "I have a problem."

But declaring I was powerless over alcohol did not make those problems disappear. I did not want to look at myself, and I was incapable of loving myself;

booze provided me an escape hatch from that existence, until I could no longer sleep at night, survive a social event, or have sex without it. I was indeed powerless, but I had lost my power to those inner voices long before alcohol came into the picture.

I do admit that I was drowning my emotions and fears in substances. Throughout the day, I ignored my fears and insecurities, blundering through my life in hopes they would not catch up with me. In the fog of nightly inebriation, I was not fully present in my desires or honest about my fears, so my sexual interactions were sometimes less than authentic. Rather than pursuing intimacy, desire, exploration, and joy, I lost myself in the consumption of alcohol, hiding always from myself. Engaging in sex only when under the influence diminished or blurred those acts and mired them in shame. I needed to take a step back from my excessive consumption in order to reboot, reassess, and recreate my personal and sexual identity.

I now see that because my power was taken away from me as a child, I consumed excessively to push away that *feeling* of powerlessness. Alcohol enabled me to forget my powerlessness, but it was not the source of that feeling. It was not the thief of my power. To regain my power, I had to look at myself, my past, my damage, and all the truths that booze helped me ignore.

I also needed help.

2. Seeking help, guidance, and love

I need loving and compassionate help to heal, to grow, and to realize my potential.

AA Step Two: Came to believe that a Power greater than ourselves could restore us to sanity.

As a child, I often lived in fear. My parents married very young and were bordering on poverty. My father, stressed out and a victim of abuse himself, would sometimes become violent. I was the only queer in a hetero-centric, sports-obsessed family. My mother, barely older than a child herself, was stuck at home in rural Maine with three kids (of the five they would eventually have), no car, few friends, and a tumultuous relationship, so she turned me into her friend and sometimes her therapist. As the third child, I was born into their well-established chaos.

My parents are also good and loving people. I am not here to cast blame on them, for they genuinely loved us and always made sure we knew that. They were at every sports game, recital, concert, parent–teacher conference, play, and accolade. They did their best, and we are close today, particularly my mother and I. But as a little boy, I became the source of comfort for a grown woman at a time I should have learned that parents are there to take care of the child. I taught myself to read signs of my dad's impending violence.

I learned to understand adults' stresses, disappointments, and financial struggles when I was too young to take on these things. Later, as I started to become aware of my sexuality, I then learned that the world found me disgusting and I should hide who I truly am.

As a result, as a young adult I felt like I had no value unless I was taking care of everything and everyone around me. I learned to believe that love means that I push myself aside and take care of you. I also absorbed the fear that even when I take care of everything, it can go terribly wrong and things can turn angry. Hate can arise for seemingly no reason, and life can become terrifying and violent.

Everyone has their story and their problems, many much worse than mine, and my life was not horrible. It was simply too confusing for a little kid, and it taught me to devalue myself and to treat myself with zero compassion. I did not start drinking excessively because I was born with some mysterious, incurable disease. At the end of each day, I no longer felt useful, so I drank to quiet the voice that told me I was useless.

In AA, I heard many stories much worse than my own. Horrible and abusive pasts that would shock anyone were something I encountered regularly in those rooms. I also heard that these people, having survived the unlivable, had a disease. I did not hear that they had abused alcohol and drugs to deal with the shit life had handed to them, but that they drank as a result of this sickness. Looking back, it baffles me.

For many years before AA, I tried to conquer my drinking problem alone and found that I could not. Like many who eventually seek out the rooms of recovery, I tried everything else first. Limit the number of drinks, never drink before a certain hour, do not mix, avoid hard liquor, take two days off, etc., etc., etc., fail, fail, fail. I tried it all alone, without ever really asking for help.

The morning of April 6, 2009, I gave up thinking that I could manage this problem alone and admitted I needed help from others. My path at the time was to go to AA. I had an ex and several friends who had gotten sober in the program, and in my brief, half-hearted encounters with AA, I had met some lovely, amazing people. I needed them. I needed help.

Though at times it may seem I'm only disparaging the program, I also freely admit that at that point in my life, it helped. These people, these generous, sober fellows took me in and showed me that I could survive without abuse of alcohol and drugs. They showed me that my life could be better than it was.

My grandfather was a drunk. The story goes that he passed out in a snowbank one night, nearly freezing to death. He allegedly made a promise to god that if he could get up and get back into the house, he would never drink again, and that is what he did. He refused to get help anywhere he might be seen and possibly recognized (apparently one of my aunts, a nurse, had to set up a secret in-home detox for him) and he never joined any sort of recovery or counseling program. He was sober and fairly miserable for the rest of his life.

I tell this story to acknowledge that while it may be possible, I cannot imagine overcoming substance abuse alone. My damaged thinking had led me to this state of my life. I needed outside forces to guide me, especially in the beginning. I needed friends and fellows who understood. The loneliness added to my self-loathing and made me unable to stop. I found a "power greater than myself" in the collective healing of others.

In the same manner that I needed positive outside influences to help my drinking problem, I needed similar help for my sexuality. Power and empowerment come in many forms and from many sources. It is up to each of us to address our issues by finding the most positive, uplifting sources thereof. As a gay man in New York, I did not need to work very hard to find some great, sexy teachers.

As I began to explore, to heal, and to separate my supposed disease from myself, I found a need to resist the narrow-mindedness of some of the groupthink in AA. In a collective, a singularity of thought can emerge, and divergence is attacked and shamed. As I heard these men telling me that I could not go to a sex club, engage in certain behaviors, or go to certain places, I began to fear that maybe I had gotten from AA what I needed, but it could not give me what I needed next.

An anti-sex mentality is predominant in Western, and particularly American, culture and certainly not found only in spaces of recovery. I highlight this problem within recovery circles because it does carry a certain circular weaponry that I find antithetical to a healthy recovery. If we continue to reiterate sex-negativity as tied to, even essential to, recovery from substance abuse, we output two very harmful messages.

First, we reaffirm a common fear that giving up drugs or alcohol means giving up a fun, joyful life. I was lucky to have a handful of beautiful, sex-positive men who pulled me aside and countered that claim with stories of very active sex lives. I also had many non-sober friends who were celebrating exploring their sexual boundaries. But I frequently encountered messages in these meetings, accompanied by nods and noises of agreement, contradicting sex-positivity.

The second message is more insidious because it is based in shame. If we tell the person struggling with substance abuse that having sex is shameful and akin to a relapse, they will be mired in that shame if and whenever they choose to have sex. That shame has been heaped upon them by society and then reinforced by those claiming to be siblings in the process of healing.

Instead of providing a safe haven and encouraging a journey back to a life without substance abuse, we impose shame and guilt on people by telling them that sex and relapse are inherently connected. When, not if, we do have sex, that is a dangerous mental space to be in. The self-loathing pushes us closer to rather than farther from abusing again, and in particular, encourages sneaking, hiding, and lying. The reality was simple: I was going to fuck. Others making me feel bad about that made me more likely to drink again, not less.

I am not naïve. I see the dangers and allure of using booze, narcotics, and mood-changers in certain environments. When we are talking about less traditional sexual experiences (sex parties, cruise bars, orgies, saunas, fetish, etc.), it is true that these worlds often involve the consumption of drugs and alcohol. I have been offered drugs and alcohol many times from anonymous sexual partners, and I freely admit there were times in sobriety when, in the height of sexual ecstasy, temptation flashed. I understand the fear: repeatedly walk into a situation where people are using and you might end up using yourself.

What we ignore with this hyperbolic focus on sex is that for a person struggling with substance abuse and a long history of self-harm, everywhere can be a danger zone. I was much more tempted to get blindly drunk while lonely and sad at home than I ever was in a bar. That is not everyone's truth, but the point is that we cannot avoid temptation. We may need to minimize that temptation while building tools to combat it, but asking sexually active gay men to avoid sex is not the answer. Avoiding life, authenticity, and pleasure is not a life worth living for many of us, so asking us to avoid sex is ridiculously narrow-minded and, frankly, detrimental.

So much sex-negativity comes from American puritanical views and from a deep, ugly fear of intimacy. I cannot count the number of times at AA I heard the same people who lauded the human connectedness found in those rooms also denounce connecting with others through sex. In or after a meeting, sober and nonsexual connection should be sought. Naked, free, sexually alive, and excited— that connection should be avoided. Yet are the participants in both experiences not seeking the same thing?

I am often quite affectionate after sex, especially if the encounter is particularly raunchy or involves fetish. I also find moments of affection during sex— little pauses, shifts in the dynamic, or intimacies that allow the exploration to be safe, human, consensual, and loving. I have found in Europe this is more the norm. I will leave the explanation of that to the sociologists, but with American and British men, this affection often shakes or frightens them, and on a few occasions, they've declared they have fallen in love with me. I can only assume that these men were so trained to separate intimacy from sex, particularly one-night stands and/or fetish sex, that the combination of the two sets off an emotional reaction.

It is not love. It is relief. I know that these declarations are not real, romantic, or even actually directed at me. It is simply the response of scared men, told they must be strong and distant, who then feel seen and safe in the presence of another person, maybe for the first time. I am not what they believe me to be in those moments; I am simply there.

One night, after having great sex in a fetish bar, a man I had been with left at the same time as me. We had played with each other and with several other men, but the night had been mostly between the two of us, and we deeply connected. We went to grab a meal afterwards. He took a bite of his cheeseburger, chewed slowly, swallowed, and said, "I think I'm falling in love with you." The couple at the table next to us thought they might have to perform CPR as I nearly choked on my falafel. I remember thinking, "Do you even know my name?!"

This extreme response to emotional vulnerability in men exerts itself in many arenas, not just sex. One of my exes was struggling with conflicting emotions about me leaving town, so he tried to start a huge fight with me because anger made more sense to him and felt safer than sadness. My brother, the victim of the majority of our father's physical abuse, only recently spoke the word "trauma" out loud about himself for the first time, at the age of forty-six. I have a dear friend who once stopped me mid-conversation on a busy street in Paris to say, "You know I love you, right?" Although I consider myself emotionally available, I was still shocked by his ability to express such intimacy on the fly and unprompted. That time, I nearly choked on an eclair, but because I believed him. And I love him, too.

American boys are taught from a very young age, that there are weak and there are strong emotions. Sadness, fear, vulnerability, and anything associated with being a victim are all signs of weakness and should be avoided. We teach boys these things in a million ways and in every forum, from parenting to school to the workplace to sex. Too often to count, we see that scene in a film or on TV where a mother turns to her young son and says, "I need you to be a man now," accompanied by emotional music. What she means, every time, is strong, fearless, and pushing his pain aside, never to be expressed. Actions are manly. Feelings are not.

As adults, men are then expected to have an emotional vocabulary using the words and feelings we were forbidden to express as children. When combined with the mixed messages of male sexuality, this contributes to, at best, emotional ineptitude and, at its worst extreme, physical or sexual violence. Men, perceiving a wrong done against him, have been taught that the only valid response to pain is anger. Anything else is weakness. When you are queer and told that you are weak and not a real man, the emotional ineptitude is caught in a hurricane of mixed messages and internal feelings, the truth slamming up against the perceived in a million ways.

We want grown men to be kind, affectionate, and emotionally honest. We teach young boys that every one of these qualities means you are feeble and stupid. What it means to be a man needs to change, and it needs to shift in the messaging about manhood and maleness that we deliver to the young. It needs to change now, before the next generation of violence begins.

The converse, the antidote, is compassion. That man who thought he was falling in love with me was not crazy. He is a product of his youth, wildly confused by the marriage of filthy sex and honest affection from a stranger. The intimacy baffled him. My ex did not pick a fight because he is broken. He simply was never, in his entire upbringing, allowed to say, "I am sad," and get a hug, so he did not know how to say the same to me. My brother is a kind, generous educator and a wonderful father who has broken a cycle of violence. It still took him three decades to admit he had been a victim and that it affected him.

At the heart of all of this is a deeply ingrained misogyny. The worst sin a man can commit is to act like a woman. Growing up closeted, I became so used to hearing insults of femininity that I still occasionally catch myself using them to this day. Yet they are violent, sexist, and damaging. How is it possibly acceptable to say things like, "Don't be such a little bitch" to someone expressing sadness, frustration, or fear? Nonetheless, it usually gets a laugh.

Some things have changed for the better, but our education of our boys remains the same. How beautiful would it be if in that movie scene, the line was, "I need you to be a man now. Cry in Mama's arms and tell me why you are hurting," accompanied by beautiful music, implying a moment of truth and sending a message that a man can talk about his feelings and fear, and accept love in response?

We all need help to undo and unlearn what has been taught to us. Instead of judging, we could help each other dismantle shame-based sexual parameters. We could embrace the wide range of sexualities that exist for gay men in recovery with respect and care.

Yes, there are some for whom sex is dangerous, driven by self-loathing, and there is plenty of support for those people. There are others who want a simple and monogamous life. That choice is overwhelmingly supported in recovery circles, even celebrated. We should also give support, love, and tools to remain healthy to the others, to the rest of us. To everyone.

Sex, whether with one person or many, can and should be a celebration of life. There are many of us who want to fuck our brains out. I wanted to shed the failures and the lost memories of blackout sex and dive into a life of sexual freedom with my senses intact. Sexual connection is equally as important to me as to those society deems acceptable. There seemed to not be much space for people like me in the rooms of AA.

I began to wonder if continued help must come from other sources. I needed help to halt my drinking problem, and up to a certain point, I found that in AA. I needed help to rediscover and love my sexuality, and for that I had to leave the rooms. I needed to go out and explore, even as those who were trying to help me with my drinking tried to stop me. So, I went and found a whole lot of help in basements and backrooms, saunas, and in the beds of strangers and friends.

I loved redefining my sexuality during that period when I was sober, being fully conscious in a room full of sweaty, horny men. I loved smelling and tasting everything dripping and spewing in those places. I thrived on being fully aware, and I floated for days afterwards on the clear memories of every thrust, suck, and spurt. I love remembering everything.

My exploration of fetishes bloomed during sobriety because I was present and making clear and decisive choices about what I wanted to try and with whom. It was, and continues to be, amazing. I could not have done it without the support and encouragement of many beautiful men living out their sexual authenticity before and with me, but I had to leave the program to find them. Luckily, I did find many, many of them.

I also learned in AA that I should remain teachable. I became confused when I heard lessons on sexuality that directly contradicted a life of joy and freedom and were the antithesis of open-mindedness. I do believe remaining available and teachable is vital to growth, but I began to realize that one must also consider the source of the lesson.

In college, one of my professors gave me some of the best advice I have ever received. He said, "You have no right to give a writer feedback on a script you don't like." He went on to explain that if you love the premise of a play and find the characters and plot interesting, your feedback can be helpful in developing that story. If you do not like the play, you have no place advising the playwright on how to improve a story you do not think should be told in the first place. You are incapable of giving useful guidance.

It is also true in life. If you do not agree with someone's path, you cannot advise them on how best to travel it. You cannot give me counsel on how to best do something you think I should not do at all.

Having admitted I needed help, my next question was, "But from whom?"

3. Following the lead of those who live how I want to live

I want to remain teachable by those who, through their lived experiences, are able to guide me.

AA Step Three: Made a decision to turn our will and our lives over to the care of God as we understood Him.

In early sobriety, my sponsor's partner casually described him as a beacon of love. I remember crying, thinking how lucky I was to have found this man to guide and help me, this person who lived as a beacon of love. I wanted that. I wanted to be that. We then all had a good laugh, myself included, at my sudden blubbering, "I want somebody to call me that!"

That same sponsor, that beacon of love, is the man who simplified step three for me. The original language of the step sounds straight off the pulpit: "Turn our will and our lives over to the care of God." It was a directive more grand than I could comprehend, let alone live out. I turned to my sponsor, confused and overwhelmed, and he said, so simply, "Oh, that just means you listen. Every time you follow a suggestion, especially if you don't understand what the result will be, you're doing step three."

Capital-G God did not need to be some bearded man in the sky or even a great and omnipotent force. Turning my will over to heal simply meant following the lead of someone who was living in a way I wanted to live. It meant following the loving advice of another at a time in my life when I could not love myself. The trick became figuring out which advice was worth following.

In the beginning, it was about drinking. Go to meetings, get phone numbers, socialize with other sober people, reach out when you are feeling afraid or triggered ... all of which I needed and used. As I became more comfortable in a life without constant consumption of booze I absorbed broader advice about living a new version of my life. Take a positive action without attachment to the results. Meditate. When you are feeling low, ask another person about their day to shift your focus away from self-pity and to activate your mind in a positive, useful way. Again, these all helped me stay sober and become more present in the world.

At a certain point, though, I began to examine the advice in relation to the source. A man twenty years sober can tell me some wonderful stories and tricks he used to stay sober. That same man might also not have a single friend outside of AA, so when he gives advice on how to rebuild a life, I do not want to follow that part of his path. And if he has never, in those twenty years, explored his sexuality, engaged in fetish, or celebrated his ability to fuck with life-affirming abandon, then his advice on sex and romance is definitively not for me.

There is a tricky thing that happens in American rooms of recovery. People can use a sober life as a shaming technique, often without realizing it. Men who disapprove of promiscuity, who have disdain for non-monogamy, or who are bitter that they are no longer in those sexual circles can use sobriety as a weapon. I often heard things like, "If you do that, you'll drink," "If you go there, you'll end up high," and even, "You can make your own choices, but if you don't follow my advice you'll probably end up back where you were, fucked up and alone."

As I began to question this connection between sex and sobriety, I decided that slut-shaming in or out of AA was simply something to ignore. Instead of asking why people were slut-shaming, I decided that their motivations were none of my business. Perhaps the man who told me "Open up that app and you might as well just call your drug dealer" was genuinely concerned for my well-being. Or maybe he was suffering from internalized homophobia. His "why" was not my concern, because his sex life was not one that I wanted. I do not believe that sex and substance abuse cannot be separated, so all I needed to know is that he was operating from a belief system I do not share. In hindsight, it seems easy, but it took time, baby steps, and a confidence I did not yet have.

There were other places I could go for guidance on sexuality, people whose suggestions I could follow. Many men in the fetish community have taught me amazing, kinky things. I learned to push my limits and explore my desires while under the protection and care of consent. I found parts of my body that I did not know existed and which have sent me into screaming, unimaginable ecstasy. I have tasted and touched and acted in ways that my earlier mind told me would be disgusting or unacceptable, and I've loved it.

There are people I go to for emotional guidance as well, including my younger sister who is one of my favorite people in the world. She has incredible emotional depth, yet this amazing ability to find humor and joy in everything. We continually laugh about the day she told me she was going to create emotional flashcards for us. We had been at some pool party—I don't remember why—that was mostly straight men except for her and me. As they got progressively more and more drunk, they were telling these terrible stories about getting in fights, getting arrested, and even one about taking a beer bottle on the head. She and I were horrified, but we kept getting it wrong.

Every time we thought we were supposed to say, "Oh my god that's awful!" the group would cheer with joy and pride at the memory of some violent brawl. I cried with laughter when she later told me that she would create flashcards to tell me which reaction I should have. "Head cracked open in a bar fight?" she shouted, then held up an imaginary card and cried, "That's funny! Good for you!" to "teach" us to have the correct reactions.

I love to make people laugh. I will act like an absolute fool if I can get someone to giggle who is feeling down. I think one of the great joys of being human is the chance to be there for one another and make one another smile. Every time I see my niece, since she was maybe four years old, I ask her, "Have you gotten a job yet?" because it is the best thing in the world watching her screech with laughter and yell back, "Uncle Adam, I'm a kid!"

Prior to 2009, my daily, excessive consumption of alcohol had drained my energy and dimmed my light. I was so often either drunk or hungover that I could no longer shine at my brightest. I have always wanted to be joyous, to love, to be kind, to help, and to care for the people in my life. Substance abuse takes up a lot of space and does not leave a lot of room. While most people in my life at that time still considered me a decent man, I knew I was not present for them as much as I could have been. What I did not realize yet was how little I was present for myself, not living my fullest, beautiful, queer life.

I do think that being queer showed us how to live in a way that straight men were not taught. I grew up in a time when it was clear to me, in no uncertain terms, that being gay was wrong and bad. God, society, and other (straight) men found my desires repulsive and my identity (a word we did not yet know) inferior. My sexual longings for male bodies was something to be hidden, lied about, and repressed.

So, when I finally refused and refuted these impositions and declared myself to be queer (at the time, gay) everything needed to be relearned. How to be proud, how to fuck, how to ignore the fear and shame so deeply ingrained in me, and how to love. We had no guidelines, no lessons, and (pre-internet) very few role models. We could only turn to our community and to our lovers for answers because only there was it safe to ask questions.

The most beautiful surprise was to realize that I was not beholden to straight rules. Over the years, being queer gave me the gift of choice, the ability to see and examine each heteronormative parameter and decide whether to accept, modify, or reject for myself. As a child, I learned to analyze and deconstruct rules and norms and adapted to those norms out of fear. Now, I could use those same analytical skills to free myself in sex, love, and self-expression.

My sexuality does not fit in a straight world because neither do I, which is sometimes easier to say than to accept and live with. But as a result, I have enjoyed sexual experiences that most heterosexuals cannot (or will not), in both quantity and variety. I, we, are able to have everything from group sex parties to making love, and we can mix and change and combine every version of sex, enjoying all of the spectrum. I have fucked men I have loved and made love to nameless men I had meant to fuck, and everything in between, often combining those in a single sexual endeavor. My queerness has been an obstacle, but it is also a beautiful gift.

I was once throwing a party with my live-in boyfriend (a couple of years before we both got sober) and my mother called as we were getting the apartment ready. I told her I had bought different types of flowers so that each vase went with the color of the walls in each room. My mom has become extremely pro-queer and supportive since my coming out, so she laughed and said, "Adam, that might be the gayest thing you've ever said." "No mom," I replied, "When I said 'Put your penis in my bum' THAT was the gayest thing I've ever said." She tried to reprimand me that I shouldn't talk to my mother that way, but she couldn't catch her breath from laughing.

Love is also different for a queer person, for many of the same reasons. I do not have to adhere to the norms. I am still deeply in love with several of my exes, a fact that often baffles my straight counterparts. And yes, I mean "in love" in every sense that the term implies except for wanting to be coupled with them. I do not have to redefine my feelings for a hetero-acceptable viewpoint, and that, too, is a gift of being queer.

I love my exes. The first taught me what love is, with all of its beautiful potential, and he continues to do so today. My next boyfriend, even though he was a deeply damaged man with whom I no longer communicate, gave me the gift of deciding for myself what is right without checking in with society. Another, who is no longer with us, showed me how to trust my instincts. My last boyfriend before quitting drinking gave me the priceless gift of forgiveness, both for myself, him, and others. My first sober boyfriend helped me to both combine and separate love and sex, and he allowed me to celebrate my independence without shame. My last boyfriend in the United States led me to acceptance of my identity and greater love for those who do not share my views. And my most recent love has shown me the true vastness of my capacity to love; he has taught me to receive his impossibly enormous ability to love in a quantity I had thought unimaginable and undeserved.

I love these men—present tense, no exceptions or explanations. There were others. This list is but a tiny fraction of the many lessons and gifts I've received. Each of these men expanded my mind, my heart, and my soul in ways my own limited perspective would not have allowed. I am grateful to each of them.

It's easy to be angry and resentful of the straight world, to indulge in my excuses to hide from intimacy. It is also valid to feel that anger. Yet on those days when I am in a more peaceful state of mind, I try to reflect on queerness and celebrate the victories over our oppressors and their shame in a quiet, more personal way, by loving other men. I have so much love for my queer siblings. The affection and kindness I have received and been allowed to give is of immeasurable value. I am proud to be queer.

We can also use these gifts, this love, and this changing world to stand with others. There is so much hate and violence in this world and we, the LGBTQI+ community, already know how to love, around, behind, and in spite of those who would rather we not exist. We can take these lessons to what is happening now, and we have (especially those of us who are white, male, and cis) a responsibility to use these gifts to stand in solidarity with those who are still fighting for themselves, for their right to exist, love, and thrive.

I find it hard to understand why I have been so loved. I am overwhelmed when I consider the generosity and care that being queer has opened me to receive. I am proud. I am queer. I am hopeful that I can, maybe, in some small way, return that love, pay it forward, and do a little bit of right and good in the world. Yet even so, I struggle every day with the deeply ingrained belief that I am not worthy of love, in spite of the massive quantity of evidence showing me otherwise. Learning to love even more, often through sex, was one of the great gifts, both of my queerness and of my sexual exploration.

The dilemma that never quite goes away for a queer person is the feeling that maybe they were right. Maybe I am disgusting and what I am doing is wrong. Society's powerful influence that promiscuity is immoral has never fully left me, even now. I can know that those lessons of hatred and homophobia are wrong, but I continue to work to unlearn them. Every sexual experience helps me to do so; but when I first got sober, this work on myself seemed insurmountable.

Because of this, we all need guidance and support from those who understand. People return to the abuse of their substance of choice for many reasons, few of them logical. We never tell people not to educate themselves, further their career, find love, or help others even though we know these pursuits can be risky and triggering. We try, instead, to support them through these discoveries and changes so they can do so safely. Why then do so many give the opposite counsel when it comes to seeking out a happy, active sex life?

Who decided that the risks associated with monogamous commitment are worth it and valid, but the risks of a broader, more open sexuality should be avoided? This is rooted in old, destructive ideas of monogamy, religion, false morality, misogyny, fear, control, and shame, not in love or even empathy. We all know that a person in recovery could relapse in a sex dungeon or in an apartment shared with their monogamous partner. Why do we have compassion for the latter, yet judgment for the former?

Had I listened to much of the advice I had been given in AA, I would not have had so many beautiful sexual experiences. I would not have many amazing friends whom I met through sexual encounters throughout the world. I might still be living in fear that my sexuality would only lead me to destroy my life again. I had to ignore and reject the shame-based counsel of people I sometimes deeply admired, and in doing so I began to discover my truer sexual self. That discovery would eventually lead me to go back and examine the sources of my damage, inflicted upon me long before I became a drunk.

Therein lies the limits of AA and therefore its limitations. The program helps people quit drinking and encourages them to repeat that "sober" behavior and, logically, stay sober. On paper it is lovely and in practice it can work, insofar as many people have gotten and stayed sober using these tools. For me, there was a limit to the usefulness of that repetition; it even blocked my self-examination and growth. I listened to the frequently repeated rhetoric that if I did not "keep coming back" and "follow this simple path" forever, I would go out there and ruin my life.

After some time, this rhetoric became detrimental. It kept me rooted in the perceived success, but did not allow for me to truly delve into my past nor to expand my perception of self and the possibilities of my future. Even in AA they say, "drinking is but a symptom."

What recovery did not do for me was ask the bigger questions, or really just the one question: Why?

Why did I drink like that? What was I trying to escape? What is the source of those terrible voices I was trying to silence and the pain I was trying to numb? What am I hiding from? What needs to heal, rather than be anesthetized by alcohol and drugs? If substance abuse is the response, what is the actual, original problem? For me, "because you have a disease" was not enough of an answer.

I learned to ask different questions by listening to and following the guidance of men who had already learned. When these were sober men who had overcome a severe drinking problem, I listened when they told me how. When these were sexually free men, sober or not, I absorbed their lessons of letting go of their shame. When these same men were using drugs to help them arrive at ecstasy, I simply did not listen to that part of their lesson.

I began learning to love my sexuality, to explore and expand it, with men who were present and connected and experienced in things I wanted to try. I let them guide me as I had my fellows in AA in regard to my drinking. I started to separate the advice from the giver by a simple examination of whether that person's choices are leading them down a path I would like to follow or not. In doing so, I can avoid judgment of the person and simply assess if they have what I want. I can still love you even if I do not take your advice, and I can even love that advice for you while simultaneously rejecting it for myself.

I was also learning to find my own ethical standards, a never-ending challenge. As I live and learn and am taught by others, I also have to decide, constantly, if I agree with the lessons. To do so, I have to always ask the question, "Who determined what is right or wrong here, and why?

4. Assessing my life within my own moral framework

I choose my own standards of right and wrong and what I want to celebrate in myself and in my sexuality.

AA Step Four: Made a searching and fearless moral inventory of ourselves.

The fourth step is where I truly diverge from the thinking of AA. Step four tells us that no matter what resentment, abuse, or wrongdoing we've experienced, we must find our part in it. Our fault. Once again, on the surface, this accountability can seem like a good thing to embrace. However, for those of us who already falsely believe that we have little inherent value and that all the wrongs in our lives are already our own fault at the core, this can be a dangerous exercise.

Raised Catholic and having a personality where I disproportionately believe that things are my responsibility, my fourth step was more of an epic novel than a list. In this process, we write down the person's name, the resentment we have, the fear/insecurity/negative feeling that it created, and then the fourth column is "our part" in the incident, relationship, or resentment. I had a fourth column that read like a criminal verdict after each and every name.

We are told to list everyone we resent. It was explained to me that a resentment, in this case, is persisting negative feelings about a person. In the traditional understanding of the word, we think of people we're angry at or people who have hurt us. In this instance, resentment includes harboring guilt or shame for acting badly toward others.

The fourth step can be an extremely painful process. My experience was a realization that the pattern of behavior was the same for each person on my list. Over and over, with person after person, I reacted with fear-driven impulses that harmed them, me, or both. It was not until years later, in therapy, that I uncovered the source of that fear; but at the time, the clarity of my repetitive behavior was shocking and saddening. Without therapy, I absorbed more shame than healing, unable to separate what was and was not my own fault.

As a person who believes any negative consequences are the result of my own failures, the notion of alcoholism as a disease provided a welcome scapegoat. I believed (because I wanted so badly to believe) that I had found the cause, this sickness, and therefore could seemingly forgive myself. In reality,

I had simply renamed what I thought of as an internal, inherent brokenness. I had found a new label for that cracked, awful piece of myself—a self that was inherently damaged and unlovable—that I could heap the blame onto. This darkness inside of me now had a name: alcoholism.

In reality, as I am now discovering, I was not born with this darkness. A child is simply not equipped to manage the things I absorbed at an age long before I was capable of understanding them. I watched and sometimes fell victim to violence I could not control or stop. I held, comforted, and even advised those that should have been my caretakers. I heard the world around me repeat, endlessly, that my sexuality (of which I was aware at a very young age) was disgusting, sinful, and worthy of shame and hatred.

I did not have the capacity to understand the circumstances of these adults or their issues, so I took it all upon myself. Solving none of it, I began to believe I was inept and unlovable. When alcohol became an available method to quiet this chaos inside of me and to diminish the voices of my self-loathing, I consumed happily, rapidly, and in increasing quantities. As these negative voices learned to push through my inebriation, I consumed more and more.

While step four did help me to see my life with some objectivity and to recognize some patterns of behavior (patterns that exacerbated and possibly prolonged my alcohol abuse) it also reinforced this extremely negative self-view. The point is to rid one's life of resentments that will cause us to return to the desire to get inebriated. But if the reason I drank so much was not others, but rather a profound disappointment in myself, where was the assessment of that?

We are also told to do a sex inventory, and in this I was very lucky to have a kind and sex-positive sponsor. In addition to times I had cheated or lied, I listed one-night stands, men whose names I could not remember, group sex, and having gone to bathhouses. "Did you cause harm?" he would ask me, over and over. "If not, cross it off."

It took years for me to understand that he was trying to help me see that the shame and fear I had absorbed from a homophobic childhood and an anti-sex society was not my own voice. He gave me a beautiful gift I was not yet ready to receive. He helped me take that first tiny step toward acceptance of my sexual self.

Many of us, when drunk and high, overcame our inhibitions and pushed our sexual limits.

Unfortunately, the use of our drug of choice became abuse of that substance, and all too often after sexual encounters we woke up with regrets. Unsafe behavior, waking up in places we did not know, massive debilitating hangovers, and fuzzy or blacked-out memories of the night before plagued our sexual experiences. Sex and substance abuse therefore became synonymous, so in getting sober, we came to fear the two as intrinsically linked. Lacking any compassion for the self, I lambasted myself as if my drunkenness and my sexuality were all one thing and all deserving of punishment.

What if the reason I was such a slut when drunk was simply because I *am* a slut? What if the alcohol and drugs allowed me to do what I wanted but what society and my own insecurities had shamed me away from? Instead of blaming alcohol for my promiscuity, what would happen if I were to embrace my promiscuity without needing chemical courage to engage?

One of my main problems with AA is this mentality of "my part." I do see some value in this exercise, as so many of us seemingly drank out of anger at those people we resented, when in fact we were often drinking to punish ourselves. Removing the myth of "everyone is against me" can be an important part of the process in arresting a pattern of substance abuse.

However, the danger here is that it does not take the next step and assess the harm I had been doing to myself or, more importantly, why.

In step four, we are asked to assess our mistakes, but we are never shown how to heal from the harm done to us for which we bore no fault. We're not told what to do when we played no part in the damage done to us, particularly as children. I was not granted compassion that it was my past pain that caused me to react in fear, anger, and shame. There was no column for that.

Instead of understanding our actions, we blame the "disease." You regularly hear at AA meetings, "I was born an alcoholic." I do not believe that is true. An abused child has absolutely no part or blame in their abuse, and their subsequent need to get drunk or high to escape that damage is not caused by a genetic, incurable disease. It was caused by violent adults.

As these statements about the nature of my problem and about my sexuality began to unravel in my mind, eventually so would the falsehoods of my own story. Long before drinking again, I began to pull away from AA as I explored my desires as a single man, toyed with more fetishes, and embraced my non-monogamy as an important part of my identity. The fear instilled in all newcomers that the moment you pull back from the program you begin to move toward life of drunkenness simply did not materialize. I did not want to be a drunk, but I did want to be free, honest, sexual, and more courageous.

Let me be clear, again, that this negativity toward a sex-positive lifestyle is far from unique to the rooms of recovery. Even today, when I say "sex-positive" many people hear "sex-obsessed." Sex-positive means simply that I find consensual sex to be a beautiful, joyous activity, no matter its form, frequency, or quantity of partners. It means in addition to loving reading, spending time with friends, traveling, the beach, dancing, and theater, I also love sex. I consider my heterosexual, monogamous friends who regularly work to enliven and continue an active sex life to be equally sex-positive even if they have only one partner.

Sex-negativity, on the contrary, is when sex is discouraged and deprioritized, often by quoting morality. The notion that becoming a true adult means "settling down" and "finding the one" runs rampant through American society, and in that construct, sex is something worth sacrificing. Even in the gay community, the battle wages between the monogamous and the sex-positive, an ongoing fight which I will never understand. When did we, a population once fighting for our sexual freedom, decide to judge each other for our sexual choices?

During the fight for gay marriage a dangerous rhetoric evolved. Queer people claimed to be "just like everybody else" and pushed the fairies, the freaks, and the sluts out of the public eye. Now, having won gay marriage, and supposedly having adopted this rhetoric only for the sake of victory, those of us who choose to reject sexual norms and heteronormativity are often still shamed for these choices. The damage to the trans and non-binary people in our community is possibly irreparable, playing out in horrifying ways nearly a decade later.

What are we fighting over? I believe very simply that if I fuck lots of people and I am not fucking you, then what I do with those others is none of your concern. You can choose to be monogamous or be a slut, or any other option that makes you happy, and I will be happy for you. Live your life and let me live mine. Both options, and the countless others in between, are valid and beautiful choices so long as all of the partners are consenting adults. Can't we all just get along?

With my first sober boyfriend, the time came to meet his family. His father is Coptic Christian (though not terribly religious) and his mother is a practicing

Muslim. I was so scared, so sure they would hate me and my gayness. After spending some time together, his father (to whom we never said "boyfriends," but I'm pretty sure he knew) and I got along beautifully. His dad is a hilarious, forceful, affectionate man, and we liked each other almost immediately.

His mom was a tougher case. She knew without a doubt that I was her son's boyfriend, and her religious convictions made her believe that in being gay, we were going against god. She was cordial, but there was a distance. I went into that situation thinking how difficult it would be for me. I quickly saw it was equally if not more difficult for her. Once we began to get along, it became even harder for her to navigate. She liked me, but she did not want her son to be with a man.

Over time, we developed a language through a silent agreement. She would treat me like her son-in-law, and I avoided being outwardly affectionate with her son in front of her. We both moved our barriers and adjusted our prejudices and found a beautiful middle ground. I knew we were more than okay the first time she yelled at me like I was one of her children. I couldn't stop laughing when she punched me in the arm in admonishment of something stupid I had done, knowing she and I were now good.

I realized then that we only see things from our own point of view, making assumptions based on our singular perspective. When I saw that she struggled with her religious beliefs against wanting me to be part of the family, I suddenly understood. It was not that she did not accept me for being gay, but rather that she needed to accept I was with her son. I could see her side of things without having to take responsibility for it. My job was not to change her, it was simply to understand her and find a compromise.

When I examine things from only my side, I miss things. When I looked at the resentments in my life and only examined my part in them, I did not see the full picture. I needed to step back further than AA asked me to do. It was necessary for me to resist this notion that everything bad that had happened to me could be traced back to my part in it. My boyfriend's mom and her prejudices had nothing to do with me. Only by realizing the tension between us was not about me and that I played no part in her preconceptions could we find a common ground and, eventually, respect and love. "That's her stuff, not mine," I thought, and in doing so I was able to give her time to get to know and accept me.

I needed to develop a language of right and wrong according to my own ethical scale. When examining my sex life after getting sober, I had immense guilt and shame about my drunken escapades in sex clubs and bathhouses, but that guilt and shame was not my own and it was far from justified. I had absorbed the messages of society and transferred them to my sobriety, reinforcing the notion that my sluttiness was a part of my "disease" and not a beautiful, valid part of myself. The association of sex and drunkenness, of alcohol and that shame, needed to be undone. When we assess the damage we have done in the world we can also, should also, consider ourselves. We must, or we cannot begin to heal.

When it came to alcohol consumption, I had great shame about that as well. I was embarrassed and horrified by each drunken escapade. As such, I was so happy to learn that I had a disease, and that the simple solution was to never drink again. I did not have the emotional acuity at the time to realize that I was yet again reinforcing my inherent brokenness. I could reframe the blame, but the fault still pointed inward.

Additionally, the universal diagnosis that a problem drinker can never consume again provides a solution, a Band-Aid, that does not address the damage. It entirely ignores the cause. It then serves to terrify and hold the person within the group repeating over and over that if you leave, if you ever let alcohol touch your lips, you will likely end up in "a hospital, an institution, or a morgue."

In the early twentieth century when *Alcoholics Anonymous* was written and the vast majority of members were pulled out of a detox or a hospital bed, perhaps this panic state of "never again or you'll die" was warranted. I do not know because I was not there. For me, and I believe for many others who drank to escape our feelings and our past, this antiquated mentality is not the best path. I do not want to eliminate the damaging reaction from my life and stop there, blaming only some inner sickness. I want to understand why and from what pain I chose to do myself harm, and I want to heal from that. I am not incurable.

All too often the greatest hurt inflicted is the repetition of self-hatred and self-harm in an unending, vicious continuation that renders us incapable of seeing ourselves as anything other than wrong and bad. I did harm others and I must look at those errors and mistakes. I must take responsibility for my actions and choices. I should also treat myself with the same compassion, love, and regret and ask for relief from the near-constant damage I did to myself.

My truth is that I am not diseased. My drinking was a reaction to my past, and in addressing my trauma I have found I can, for the time being, drink without harming myself. I also know, after twelve years of sobriety, that if my old issues flare up and I begin to drink again in an unsafe manner, I can stop.

My sex life is also not sick. It is not wrong. My sexuality is beautiful, and you may not like it, but the world no longer gets to approve or disapprove of who I am. Not anymore.

Unfortunately, if I stated these things in AA, particularly that I was not sure about this notion of disease or that I did not have a part in certain of my resentments, the reaction was extremely negative and sometimes aggressively so. I could not continue to heal in that environment, because healing requires compassion, not conformity.

I began to wonder if I was still safe in those spaces.

5. Sharing my desires and fears with those who care about me

I need compassion, from others and for myself, to truthfully examine my life.

AA Step Five: Admitted to God, to ourselves, and to another human being the exact nature of our wrongs.

In AA, we generally do step five with our sponsor because the step instructs us to share our step four list with another alcoholic. It should be a person in AA that we trust and who will listen with the experience of having made many of the same choices. In this, we hopefully find freedom and forgiveness of self. All of our terrible secrets are brought out into light and spoken aloud. The sponsor, in this case, listens and is still there in your life at the end of the process.

The idea in doing a fifth step is to share your fourth step in a private, one-on-one setting. The process can be both healing and uplifting in that we all, particularly those of us with a history of drug and alcohol abuse, have shame about things in our past. Saying those things out loud to another human being who does not walk away in disgust is lovely. It can teach us that our past does not need to destroy our present.

I was very lucky to have the sponsor I found. I have heard fifth step horror stories—people spending days on end unpacking their entire lives, childhoods, regrets, and shame with a person who is woefully unqualified to unearth these psychologically damaging reveals. I have talked to many members who came out of their fifth step proclaiming their sex inventory had shown them just how terrible they had been. I heard these stories, still wanting to follow all guidance but already beginning to question some of its validity, and I remained quiet.

Later, I would often go back to thank my sponsor for his patience, his kindness, and his lack of judgment. Before my fifth step, he looked me directly in the eyes and said, "I am not your therapist. That's not what this is. I highly recommend going to therapy if that's what you need, but that is not me. You will share these things with me to get them off your chest, and that's it. Clear?" And that is what he did. He listened.

In one of my early relationships with a man several years older than me, I discovered he had invented his entire past and life story, as he was deeply damaged from years of violence and abuse as a child. Before that discovery, when we fought (always drunk), he would sometimes physically attack me, once so badly that the police showed up. I went to my first bathhouse with that man who had abused me. I tested out non-monogamy with him. I explored early steps into role-play and fantasy with him. We were drunk every time. He would later shame me and punish me for being such a slut, telling me I was a whore who always "wanted it" even though he had been there, doing these things with me. His was the first name on my step four list.

When I shared "my part" in this with my sponsor, announcing my drinking had made things worse and that I had engaged in these fights, he stopped me. He looked so sad. "Adam," he said, "his lies and his abuse were not your fault. Your only 'part' in this is that you are still carrying it with you and you've been drinking over it for years."

I remember tears flowing down my cheeks as I stared at him and listened to his words. I wish I could say that it was a moment of finally forgiving myself, but it was not. I wept because I could not understand what he meant. I cried because I did not believe him. I thought it was all my fault and that I had driven that man to his violence against me. I also felt enormous guilt for having left him to protect myself, thinking I had abandoned him.

In the fifth step, we try to unburden ourselves; but simultaneously the repeated messaging of AA is that we must examine our part or we will drink or use drugs again. I could not shake the notion that I had caused and therefore deserved my ex's anger, shame, and emotional and physical abuse. Both my drinking and my sexuality were the cause, the problem, and therefore the parts of myself that needed to be stopped, squashed, and removed. Unfortunately, the rhetoric of AA served to reinforce that idea. Doing the work of step five by sharing my fourth step seemed a little bit like showing your homework to the teacher, and I desperately wanted all of the "my part" answers to be correct.

There is a subtle but highly damaging aspect to this process. It seems like forgiveness and unburdening, but the subtext (sometimes overtly stated) is that the choices made before you got sober were bad choices, and now you can make better ones. It mires the entire life prior to finding the light of AA in shame. For those of us who drank or abused drugs to avoid an already overwhelming self-loathing, the process does not heal. It reiterates that we are sick, bad people, and then traps us in a belief that our only hope is the twelve steps.

I needed to untangle my desires from my shame, and the twelve steps did not help. Even though my kind, loving sponsor tried to circumvent and modernize some of it (and gently suggested therapy, more than once), the other messaging I heard in the literature and in the rooms stayed strong and held fast to my already enormous proclivity for self-abuse. I already believed that I was a broken and damaged person, and finding my part in every negative event in my life served to reinforce that belief.

My sponsor did not, in any way, reinforce that shame, but he could not undo the voices in the rooms, in society, and in my head, at least not at first. He did—and I am so lucky in this regard— lead by example. He would casually mention a sexual massage meet-up group he had joined. We would hear stories of somebody else's sexual adventurism, and he would laugh and smile with approval and joy. He and a few others seemed to have this hidden pact, saying nothing in meetings when members talked about the horrors of their sexual past. But then, almost in secret, there were those of us who wanted to be sexually free and thought the connection to our drinking or drug problem was nonsense. These men saved me.

In meetings, when we tell our story, we are asked to share "what it was like" (when abusing my substance of choice), "what happened" (to change my life), and "what it's like now" (that I am sober). It is a simple formula to keep the speaker on track, sharing their "experience, strength, and hope" in a way that is relatable to everyone in the room and hopefully serves to inspire. The before, the change, and the after of a life with and then without substances is told so that others might see that recovery is not only possible, but desirable.

The trap of this formula is that it falsely divides the self, a life, into two persons, when in reality there is only one. I indulged deeply in the myth of an "old" and "new" Adam. I told a story of a man alone, selfish, and sinning who found recovery and himself. The reality was that all of my self existed on both sides of that recovery divide, and yet I spoke as if the earlier version of me were a fabricated, drunken lie, and this new person was unencumbered and authentic.

A few years into recovery, having been frequently asked to speak at meetings, I began to feel a gnawing sense of falseness about my so-called truth. I had become quite good at telling my story, my theater background coming into play and my need for approval shining strong. I crafted a beautiful tale of woe and redemption that usually resulted in laughter, tears, and someone asking me to speak again at another meeting. Something about it, though, did not feel right.

Was the love I had felt for the men before sobriety was not real? It had felt real. Was all of the sex just acting out and not truly desired? It couldn't be, because those desires were still present and strong. And (the big question) other than eliminating drunkenness and hangovers from my life, was I any better of a person? Not being drunk every night and hungover every day was certainly an enormous improvement on my quality of life. But had I, as a human, evolved?

The truth is, even before sobriety, I was kind. I was generous. I loved my friends deeply and I took my work seriously. I found myself in meetings downplaying or erasing these qualities from the "what it was like" part of my story to serve a dramatic end in my tale of redemption. As this came into my consciousness, I began to speak less and less in meetings, feeling like a fraud. On the outside, in the real world, I began to wonder what else I might be rewriting from my past.

I remember that when I first came into recovery, I was horribly ashamed when I would run into someone I knew from the outside world at a meeting. That person, inevitably, would put a hand on my shoulder and say, "Adam, you do know I'm here for the same reason as you?" Many years later, I ran into a sober fellow at a sex party. His eyes widened and he looked as if he were about to bolt. I put my hand on his shoulder and gave back that little gift. I had heard the same messages as him and I understood his fear.

I could not talk openly about my sex life in American, gay AA meetings, where we can talk about literally anything else. There in those rooms, I often felt shamed for my unsober thinking and behavior, and more than once I was accused of potentially triggering a relapse in others. It was a joy to have sober sex, but I often could not express that joy with many sober men because somewhere along the way, the groupthink, deeply rooted in American culture, decided that enjoying an exciting, healthy, active, multiple-partner sexual existence was in contradiction to sober behavior. It was how we acted "before."

I was lucky in that my desire to more deeply explore my sexuality grew as my desire to get drunk diminished. I was becoming less dependent on the approval of everyone who was sober, choosing instead to move closer to those people living a life that resembled what I also wanted. I had begun to forge my own path, separating my "disease" from my personality one piece at a time. Even so, I did hide much of my sexual escapades except from a few close, like-minded friends, and almost never openly discussed them in meetings.

What I found in my sexually promiscuous circles was compassion and understanding. These queer people wanted to celebrate and thrive in a sexually active life, and I watched them ignore the world's condemnation and own their desires. When sharing my sexual past in AA (and elsewhere), I was met with either disgust or a condescending happiness that I was no longer that man. Among these sex-positive queer men, I found joy, admiration, and an offer to try new things.

Two years into sobriety I ended up in a relationship with a partner, Amine, with whom I began to experiment with, discover, and expand my sexual choices. My experience up to this point with non-monogamy had been fairly limited, and mostly occurred when that ex and I would decide to bring in a third or go to bathhouses and cruising bars—but only when drunk. As Amine and I moved toward coupling, we discussed having an open relationship as a future possibility. We shared the belief that it was a beautiful idea—having multiple partners and sharing our sexual selves with others without jealousy or possessiveness—but in the beginning neither of us felt yet ready to take that leap.

As time went on, the details of our situation changed when Amine found himself with an offer to spend six months abroad. Again, very much on the same page, we agreed it was time to open up the relationship rather than choose celibacy or, more likely, cheating. That same week, we had our first threesome, and it was fantastic.

Sober sex was wildly different. Aware of my partner, having (both) chosen to do this sober, we had sex with another man, kissed him goodnight, and fell asleep in each other's arms, happy. I knew I could let Amine go across the ocean and enjoy an active sex life while I did the same in New York. I will always be grateful to that man who came into our bed and opened another door for me toward sexual freedom.

After his return from abroad, Amine and I began to explore even more. We went to leather bars and rediscovered sex shops and saunas. We engaged in more threesomes, had separate sex while in the same city, and even took on a third semi-boyfriend for a few weeks. There were, of course, struggles and jealousy and a few difficult reassessments of the "rules," but overall it was fantastic. With this other sober man, our decisions were conscious and our lines of communication always open. Mistakes were just that, and we could be honest about our desires as we slowly dismantled our previous attachment to heteronormative sexual constructs.

He and I deconstructed our fears, one at a time, by regularly revising our rules. Fairly quickly, we let go of the obvious, old thinking that was imposed upon us by sex-negative norms. Early rules like "don't ask don't tell" and "never the same person twice" were dropped. This life was something we were sharing, so why not talk about it? We both knew it was impossible to control the other person's feelings, so why have a rule that attempted to do just that? Eventually, we even let go of rules like "never in our apartment" and "nobody we both know." Those were more difficult because they hit closer to home.

It was not always easy. Sometimes the rules changed because one of us broke that rule, and a difficult discussion followed. Even so, because these discussions were not fueled by drugs or alcohol, we almost always spoke with love. We admitted our own and acknowledged the other's fears, but gently prodded each other away from pretending our anger was anything more than being afraid. When the romance had eventually run its course, our honesty turned the relationship into one of the greatest friendships of my life and one that continues today. The lasting effects of the relationship on my sexual identity and confidence are invaluable.

Yet if I hadn't been given that support—from my lover, my sponsor, my sex-positive friends—would I have been so safe in that exploration? Could I have done so without excessive alcohol consumption if the groupthink shame accompanied me into those beds, bars, and bathhouses? For those without such support, which is many single gay men in American AA, are the warnings of that "slippery slope" helping or hurting? I am able to speak from only my own experience, but I can say that at the time, I had to reject the groupthink, ignore the shame, and discard much of the rhetoric in order to find my own truth, path, and sexual joy. I needed the love of my open-minded fellows to do so.

In my life today, I find myself surrounded by people who know who I am and who accept all parts of me. I have many monogamous friends and sex-positive sluts in my circle. I have friends who are sober and those who are not, ranging from non-drinkers to problem drinkers. I know artists and accountants and salespeople and doctors. I have friends born all over the world and who speak dozens of languages, and I have people whose lives range from ideal to disastrous. The common thread is a shared compassion and a celebration of our differences. The quality amongst all of them is that we are there for each other, whether or not our challenges and choices are experientially relatable in each other's lives. The common denominator is kindness and love.

Life is hard. It is also beautiful. We are all evolving and changing, fucking up and growing, and through it all we are just trying to do our best. I am so lucky to have friends who love me and let me love them without us needing to impose our desires or choices upon each other. They allow me to make my own choices and often want to hear my stories that vary so wildly from their own. Most importantly, we leave each other to decide what is right or wrong for each person, with compassion and space to change one's mind. They are my recovery now from my earlier life because they respect my ethical scale even when it doesn't match their own; they want only my happiness, and I want the same for them.

When I or they make a mistake, we respond first with, "Are you okay?" instead of "Why did you do that?" I need to share with my friends and lovers the mistakes I have made and the things that cause me fear. What I do not need is someone to ask me to find my part, my fault, in life's challenges. I do that excessively, all by myself. I need compassion, love, and often a little help to stop being so hard on myself. I also give those gifts to others.

With that support, love, and openness, I could finally begin to explore and create the life I wanted to live.

***

It is important at this point that I stop and acknowledge my privilege as a major factor in my capacity and freedom to take this journey. I am queer, and as a result of that I have certainly suffered discrimination, shaming, persecution, and even violence. I have been attacked, seen my rights publicly, hatefully debated on hundreds of occasions, and been the victim of discrimination professionally and personally. I know what it is to be marginalized and abused because of my identity.

I am also white, cis, male, thin, American, and non-disabled. Over the years, we have seen a steady decline in the anti-gay discrimination of my youth, but people of color, trans people, immigrants, and people who are fat or have disabilities continue to be victimized by hate, discriminatory systems, social macro- and microaggressions, and violence, both physical and mental. My identity as gay or queer certainly has its challenges, but in significantly decreasing frequency in today's world. My other identities shroud me in extreme privilege that often outweighs my sexual identity. I am, undoubtedly, a beneficiary of white privilege.

In sexual spaces, my privilege granted me freedom to explore. Racism is very present in the white gay community, and when a Black man enters those spaces, he is often seen and treated as "other," either with suspicion or fetishization. I do not have disabilities, so my freedom of mobility in non-accessible spaces and the fact that my body is considered to be as it "should be" place me in the center and the norm. I am thin, and while there are certainly many men in the fetish and leather world who are not into that look, I am told, kindly, that I am not their type. I am never labeled as disgusting. I am also cis and appear to be so, which is, for many, a primary, discriminatory requirement to also be seen as sexy. The prejudices of the outside world definitely diminish inside the sex-positive communities, and many in those communities are doing incredible work to further break down those barriers, but there is still much work to be done.

I have felt deep shame and guilt, especially in the beginning of my sober, sexual journey. However, I was rarely afraid for my safety. I have worried, often, about what people might think of me and how they might judge me and treat me. I have not ever had to worry if white people's sexual prejudices would combine with their other -isms to drive them to hurt and physically harm me. Homophobia can certainly manifest as violence, but homophobia plus racism, transphobia, and/or misogyny is a whole other level of scary.

I say this to acknowledge that any reader who is not white, cis, thin, male or who has a disability will have enormous obstacles and challenges which I did not experience. Much of what has been written up this point has been about me rejecting norms and expectations and finding the freedom and courage to experiment and to discover my own sexual self. In many instances, I did nothing to earn, gain, or learn to find that courage. Society just handed it to me.

***

6. Living in this world more closely aligned with the person I desire to be

I can create the life I want while continuing to keep away from choices that will cause me harm.

AA Step Six: Were entirely ready to have God remove all these defects of character.

It will probably surprise some people to know that I love step six, both then and now. The original phrasing is awful, hyper-religious, and deeply couched in Christian shame. The psychological implications that your substance abuse is a defect of character rather than a survival mechanism in response to trauma borders on horrifying. The words, "have God remove all these defects of character" should be rewritten, and don't get me started on the beloved phrase, "This is the step that separates the men from the boys." Yet I found an intent behind this step that I love: I want to live a better life and be a better human in the world.

At the end of step six in *The Twelve and Twelve* (as the book that outlines the steps and traditions is affectionately called) there is one sentence that landed in my soul, and it may be the reason why I stayed in AA for so long. It resonated within me in a way that changed my sobriety and aligned my ideals, helping to grant my desire to heal more power than my desire to punish myself. It states, "This is the exact point at which we abandon limited objectives and move toward God's will for us."

My idea of god or a higher power is inconcrete and ever changing. I like the idea of believing there is a higher force of benevolence. I see the sun set over the sea and feel that something greater exists, and I also understand the Freudian notion that our need for a god is childish fantasy, a refusal to accept that we are unparented in the world. Ultimately, I just do not know.

My spiritual practice resembles more of a yard sale than a religion. There are elements of Christianity, Judaism, Buddhism, and Islam that I apply to my sense of ethics. I have deeply loved deities across the spectrum, from praying to Ganesh in Hinduism to presenting gifts to Chango, Ochun, and Yemeja in the Ifa and Santerian traditions. I have meditated with my ancestors and visited mediums to connect with my spirit guides.

I believe in all of it, and none of it, because it all feels both beautifully connected and wildly insufficient up against the enormity of the universe. I often think that all of these practices might just be limited pathways attempting to move closer to something greater, but that each is an inadequate method to understand what we cannot comprehend; therefore no one choice holds any superiority for me. Tomorrow, I may not believe that at all.

What I do believe consistently is that there is a force *within* each of us that wants us to heal. Our humanity, our spirit, our soul—whatever word you use—wants us *not* to destroy ourselves. That force, love, and compassion exists within each of us and within others. It is often easier to direct that healing, loving light toward those we care about than toward ourselves, for whom we should also care. Even my substance abuse, though detrimental, was an attempt to protect myself from the pain and disappointment of a child. I have no idea if an external god exists, but to heal myself I do not need a god. I only need that part of me that wants the pain to stop.

When connecting to that source, I can see that my objectives have been terribly limited. I am often driven by fear and even terror, so I often only see two choices in reaction to a situation: fight or flight. I can either aggressively attack the problem, or I can run away. The idea that these are the only two choices that exist is simply untrue, so to abandon that idea of "limited objectives" opens up the world and life to infinite possibilities.

We tend to divide the world and our choices into a series of binary options. Male or female, career or family, good or evil, monogamous or slut. By limiting our perspective to these two extremes, we narrow ourselves and our objectives to only those that fit this dichotomy. Even if I was unsure about my belief in a god, I began to see that life and that force of love within me have so many more options outside of the two I instinctually see. By unlimiting my way of looking at the world and being open to its infinite options and objectives, myriad beautiful alternatives emerge.

The practice of finding these unlimited objectives is easier than it sounds. When I am feeling in conflict about a decision or struggle, I ask myself, "What other possibilities exist?" When I was sober and wanted to get drunk, my first thought told me I could either get wasted or suffer through the feelings I was having. The reality is that I could call someone, go out and do something without alcohol, watch my favorite movie, take a walk, write ... I had many other choices other than drink or suffer. I now apply this question to other things. When I take a step back, there are almost always more than two choices.

When it came to substance abuse, understanding this limited, binary instinct within myself was vital. My mind tells me that I must either "win" at whatever unreasonable, self-imposed level I have irrationally set as the bar, or I must disappear, drowning myself in something that takes me away. Finally understanding this automatic reaction, where I see only two choices, helped me to diminish the inevitability of the latter, knowing I would never live up to the standards of the former. Instead of "how do I win?" I can ask myself "what other options exist?" and a world of unknown choices opens up to me.

I now see that the entire premise of AA is based on binary thinking. Either you are completely substance free or you are in a relapse. There is no room for harm reduction. There is no space to try anything other than a single choice of total sobriety. It is the only option.

When it came to sex, eliminating this binary also changed my world. I had allowed myself to be subjected to the thinking of "good" and "bad" sex, things that I "should" and "should not" do. With the help of step six, my mind opened up to infinite possibilities through an incredibly simple mindset: I should try things before I decide if I do or do not like them. This childish, binary, predetermined judgment on certain sexual acts was nonsense, and I found myself enjoying so many new things, many of which I once thought I would never do.

I began to see that in my exploration of non-monogamy, the sexual shaming, disgust, or misinformation of those insisting a sex-negative life is the only choice are not my concern. They are too limited in their thinking. I truly love and admire the many beautifully open-minded monogamous people who do not believe that their choice needs to be the choice of any person other than their partner. I also love their monogamy. A connection with another human can take many forms, and a monogamous relationship is only one option. I can seek within myself and explore with others all of the possible choices.

Several years after I had rejected monogamy and experimented with some fetish (mainly leather and light bondage), I found my mind opening up even more. I started to wonder about sexual acts that I didn't judge, but that I thought I did not want to do myself. Was I actually running from shame? Did I really think, "Do what you like but that's not for me!" Or was I ashamed to admit that some of those things actually turned me on, and I was just afraid to try them? I was perhaps more afraid that I would like them.

The joy of not being drunk or high when exploring new forms of sex is the pleasure and safety of conscious choice. Perhaps more importantly, the next morning, without "I was so drunk last night," there is nothing to blame for the choices one has made. There is no haze or ability to hide behind the drugs or alcohol. You are beautifully left with the knowledge that you consciously and actively chose what happened the night before.

I began to ask myself, why can my journey in recovery not celebrate that? If there are things, activities, places that others need to avoid, fine. But which of those danger zones are on my own list because I agree? And which are there because I easily adapted the warnings of others when their "do not do" list coincided with my shame and fear?

One night in Paris, I was in the basement sex area of a fetish bar. I had engaged in multiple sexual acts with this one guy, and the sex had been really good. I had seen him there before that night and had seen him engage in some fetishes that I had not yet tried. I came around a corner and there he was again. We had already fucked each other and tasted every part of each other's bodies, but he pulled me to him again and we began to kiss and fondle one another.

He became very aroused, as did I. As we kissed, I felt him moaning in my mouth, and then felt a warm liquid on my leg. I thought he had cum, and I looked down to see, but there was only a tiny bit of clear liquid on my thigh. I looked at him; he smiled, and then he pissed a little bit more on my leg. He tilted his head with a gesture that asked, "Do you like it?" I dropped to my knees and he let loose, pissing all over my body and in my mouth, and I then sucked him until he came. He offered to buy me a drink afterwards, and said nothing when I ordered a seltzer.

In the fetish community, with rare exceptions, these men know how to ask for consent. They can use their bodies, their eyes, their hands, and their genitals to inquire if you like something and if you want more. They sometimes do so without words so as not to ruin the moment, but there is another, beautifully intimate element to it. They tell you that "no" is okay. They often want to push your limits, yes, but it is not what the outside world thinks. In my experience, these men wanted to take me into places I had not been, but they invited me, never forced me. And so I was safe and turned on, sometimes scared, but always in my own choice, knowing that I could ask it to stop without resistance or shaming.

That respect for consent had been largely the same for me concerning drugs and alcohol in these spaces. I have been offered everything from G to meth, and countless drinks. I rarely felt any pressure to consume. To be honest, turning down wine at a dinner party when the host insists, repeatedly and in front of everyone, that "just one glass of wine won't hurt!" came with infinitely more pressure than saying, "No, thank you" to meth in a sex dungeon.

Yet nobody tells a sober person not to go to dinner. Instead, when it comes to socially acceptable activities, AA teaches you tools and tricks to get around those obstacles, because nobody wants to live a life isolated from sharing a meal with friends. Why not do the same with sex? When you are aroused and a beautiful man offers you something, you might want to partake. Let's talk about how to not do that and still suck his dick. Again, I found that AA presented only a binary option: you cannot go there if you want to stay sober. Stay away good, go there bad.

I should point out that crystal meth was not my drug of choice. Meth is a terrible drug, deeply addicting and highly destructive. I am not speaking from that point of view It is trickier ground to navigate than alcohol, and a realm I do not know. I cannot give any experiential advice on sex for meth abusers.

That said, should we necessarily condemn recovering meth users to a sexless life? Did many of them not engage in drug use to have the courage they needed to express themselves freely in their sexuality? If so, is it not similarly precarious to then announce to a sober meth addict that sex is and will always be dangerous? Although I agree that, for many, a period of time away from certain situations is possibly necessary to quit using, I do not accept the universal declaration that non-traditional sexual experiences must be avoided forever. I know several former meth users who are very sexually active, and I wish there were more examples of post-meth sex-positivity and a lot less shame.

With alcohol, meth, or any other abuse of a substance it is of course necessary to be careful, to wade back into possibly triggering experiences with trepidation. With communication, with support, and with acknowledgement that many of us used our substances to free our inner sluts, we can find our way back to sexual freedom. We are able—I have been able—to engage in our filthiest, sexiest, most out-there sexual fantasies, and it is entirely possible to do so without abusing a substance to get there.

If I had let the thinking of much of AA's group mentality guide me, I might have continued to live in the same fear that drove me to drink so much. I had to force myself to not limit myself to what others determined to be sober or not-sober behavior. Perhaps your sobriety and your sex life look different than mine, and that is just fine. For me, a life without sexual exploration, excitement, and proliferation is a life that I would only choose if I continued to hate myself, and continuing that self-hatred brings me closer to the risk of substance abuse.

We are told that because many people imbibe where public sex occurs, we must entirely avoid those places. My own version of step six showed me that I can choose to go to those places without chemical enhancement. It is close-minded to believe otherwise. I can have the freedom of public sex without self-harming if I abandon the limited perspective that the two must coincide.

Most of my time is spent doing things other than sex, and this idea of unlimited objectives applies to it all. If I open my mind to explore all of the choices and possibilities that exist (rather than what first comes to my mind) I find myself with infinitely more options. I want to be kind. I want to love deeply. I want to travel and explore and learn. I want to speak multiple languages and try so many things. I want to have a vibrant, active sexual existence and identity. I want to try things that frighten me with an open mind, free from preconceived notions that are not my own. I want to be a complete, courageous, loving, sexual, funny, gentle, strong person in this world.

This idea of unlimited objectives also applies to how we see and treat others. That man who pissed on me for the first time was drunk when he did so. He was frequently in that fetish bar. Binary thinking could easily make you (and me) assume certain things about him. I later found out he is also a brilliant photographer and a deeply sensitive artist. Unlike his stunning photographs, life is not black and white and the initial impression you have of a person is not the whole of that person.

My choices are not limited so long as I am honest, compassionate, and open to what life has to offer. I can align my life with these values if only I allow myself to do so. I can also do so safely, as long as I connect to that source within and those without that want me to heal, to grow, and to thrive without doing harm to myself.

In that, I can find new joy and strength.

7. Drawing upon positive influences and sources of strength

I want to walk in the world seeking and giving pleasure and joy. These are not defects.

AA Step Seven: Humbly asked Him to remove our shortcomings.

Approaching step seven, after I had been sober for a bit, I struggled even more with this notion of an Adam-before and Adam-after. In particular, I needed to reject the notion that I had lived a life of self-centeredness, an idea that is often repeated in the rooms and in the texts. The belief that the person abuses drugs or alcohol out of selfishness is a grave misunderstanding of substance abuse and addresses these issues with an astounding lack of compassion. As we work these steps on ourselves, and compassion for the self is perhaps the most difficult to muster, this notion of failure and redemption is destructive.

And don't get me started on the capital-H masculine "Him" ...

It would not be until much later that I began to understand that considering myself defective was nothing more than another way to avoid addressing what was really going on. In the seventh step prayer, we are taught to talk to our version of god and say, "I pray that you now remove from me every single defect of character which stands in the way of my usefulness to you and my fellows." Praying to a higher power to "remove" my defectiveness once again reiterated the idea that I was inherently broken, rather than consequentially damaged.

I had to abandon most of this prayer because it reinforces shame and self-loathing. Drinking was an escape from my perceived character defects. To double down on those defects without any compassion for myself and then to label drinking as yet another defect was not a long-term solution, was not healing. My abuse of alcohol and occasionally drugs was not a shortcoming or a failure. I do not need to pray away these things. I need to address them with a healthy, open mind.

What I could take with me, could incorporate as part of my healing, was the notion that excessive drinking diminished my usefulness. When I was drunk every night and hungover every day, I was less capable of being present and helpful. There was not, however, a pre-sober Adam who did not care about my fellows. I was not defective; I was tired. Being a drunk and constantly running away from your past is exhausting behavior. I have always, sober or drunk, cared deeply about supporting the people in my life.

I lived in a constant state of disappointment in myself; therefore, I ended every day by drowning those feelings in booze. Logically, I then woke up every day groggy, hungover, or sometimes still drunk, meaning I was then less capable in my daily life ... so I failed again ... so I drank again. The cycle fed upon itself until I was thirty-three years old, drinking alone in my apartment and miserable.

I want to be kind and useful. I want to be generous, available, and supportive. Excessive alcohol consumption diminishes my capacity to be the man I want to be.

It took me time to realize that my "usefulness" is also sexual. Connecting with other human beings on a non-verbal level and exploring desire and pleasure can be a force of good. Society taught me to be ashamed of this, whereas having explored an active, adventurous sex life without being drunk or high showed me its beauty. For me, and for the men I am with, this expression of self, this enjoyment and discovery of our bodies, and even the participation in fetish that allows us to act out our fantasies in a shared, consensual space, is vital. I want to give this gift to other men and I want to love myself enough to receive it from them.

I also have to be very careful to avoid certain thinking, to avoid confusing "useful" with "valuable." I have done a lot of work, post-AA, to remember the value I place on others and try to apply that to myself. I am useful by making someone laugh. I am useful by spending time with people I care about and who care about me. I am useful every time I am present for a friend or lover, whether in silly banter or deeply personal support. I am useful simply by existing, as are you. I need to remember that useful means being there for you, not saving you or solving all of your problems.

My sponsor used to frequently say, "Put down the bat and take off the cape." The bat was the one I used to bash myself for failing to live up to my insane expectations. The cape was my superhero costume; I was convinced that I needed to save the world, one person at a time. It became a running joke between us, and it stuck with me. I check in with myself even today on this, because if I am holding the bat or wearing the cape again, I am not in a healthy space.

The work to get away from considering myself defective happened over time, and certainly not easily. Long before I became the active slut I am today, I was out with friends in New York, just three or four months without a drink. This was the first time I had gone sober to a gay bar with a dance floor. I was absolutely terrified. I could not remember ever having danced sober. Backlit bottles of booze and a roomful of gay men overwhelmed my senses, but I found safety in a group of gay, sober friends who had all been there before.

Still, on the dance floor, I froze. Without alcohol, it felt as if I did not know how to move. I could not remember how to dance. My friend Dan came up behind me, putting his hands on my hips. He swayed me to the music, and gently spoke into my ear. "Just move a little. Feel the beat," he said, "It will come back." He knew. I moved with him. I cannot imagine how awkward and silly we must have looked, but by the end of the night, I was laughing and dancing on my own. Within a few weeks, I was free again on the dance floor, maybe more so than I had ever been when drunk.

Dan danced. He had a life which included being packed in a room full of gay men, sexually charged and moving to the music. He was living a part of life that I missed, that I wanted back, and that scared me. The voices of many men crying out, "Don't go there!" were ringing in my ears, but Dan whispered louder than they yelled, or maybe I heard him because the guidance was coming from a source living a life I desired. I did not want to get wasted. I wanted to dance.

I did not know it at the time, but that moment on the dance floor helped to crack open the door to another part of me. To dance in a gay bar was the first step toward being a sexually active gay man again and the knowledge that I could do so without chemical enhancement. I wanted to dance, and I wanted to fuck.

I return often to the idea of the force within me that seeks joy instead of harm. Whether I call it love, or light, or a deity, or the universe in any given moment does not matter. It is all of these and none of these. But whatever that force, it does not hate me or think I am defective. It loves me because it *is* me.

My higher power is love and joy, happiness and light. It wants to remove nothing from me, and certainly not those things society or AA considered defective. My higher power wants me to heal from my past and live in a way where I do not cause myself harm.

Connecting to that higher power can be music, dancing, and friends. It is sometimes quiet meditation. It is often the kindness of others or my own kindness for them. A good meal, a nap, traveling, laughter, and therapy are all forms of prayer for me because they are all acts of self-goodness. Sex is definitely part of that power; the ecstasy that I and my partners experience during sex is exactly what I mean by healing, joy, and light.

Those negative voices in my head are the opposite of that power. Every time I absorbed the belief that I am inherently broken or sick, I was walking away from that light, never toward it, and never toward healing. That part of my past that is terribly vocal inside my head in the present, the thing that makes me feel ashamed when I have done no harm, is the antithesis of my higher power. It labels me as a failure and tells me I do not deserve love. It makes me question every choice, especially those that feel good and bring joy, because it also tells me I do not deserve happiness.

Labeling my choices before sobriety as "defects of character" once again lumps together all things done when drunk as part of a disease called alcoholism. It leaves no room for the possibility that I had absorbed so much pain and shame that I could not figure these things out without the lubrication of a mind-altering substance. Rather than relying on a negative self-assessment, I can lean into usefulness to figure out who and what I want to be in the world. I found that a person can be both a promiscuous lover of sex and a compassionate friend.

I am a good friend and a proud slut, and both are beautiful. The two are only in opposition insofar as I allow them to be (or allow the voices of others to tell me so), but I began to see that neither should be labeled as a defect, and both are Adam. I am also still that scared, gay child from rural New Hampshire. I always need to return, in order to be who I want to be in the world, to compassion and love for myself. I pray that my higher power elevates and celebrates those parts of me, and never removes them.

I can only move toward that strength and light if I remember that I am subject to the dangers of my own thinking. Damaged by experiences of my past, I can take the concept of being useful, helpful, and supportive to an extreme that tells me if I am not constantly those things, I do not deserve love. I do deserve love, every moment of every day.

My value, my usefulness, is not marked by numbers of days sober, by professional accolades, or by how helpful I am to you right now. I am useful and valuable because I am funny and kind. I am reliable. I am loving. I am sexual. During my time in AA, I sought applause at my day count and accomplishments at work to prove I was worthy of being a human in this world. Now, I try to know that I am always worthy and to remember that my sources of strength come by relating to other humans, in a hug, in fucking, or in sharing a glass of wine and discussing life.

AA is not equipped to address these larger, deeper, older issues and obstacles. For me the program was a lifeline, a community, and a safety net. Recovery allowed me to clear my head and clean up the mess of my life, but it did not dissolve those older problems, and it did not answer (or even ask) the real questions. At a certain point, it told me to stop asking, to "turn my will over" and just accept that I was diseased and could never drink again. That is the point where AA overextends its reach and arrests growth. That is the point where it does harm.

It was sex that first opened the door to asking myself those questions. People in AA said, "Don't go to bars" and "Don't be around anyone who does drugs" and "Don't engage in behavior related to your past." And so as I dabbled in some of these ill-advised behaviors without drinking, these warnings began to unravel for me. I wanted to meet non-sober friends out in their bar of choice. I wanted to dance, go out to dinner, travel alone, and see live performances. And I wanted to be in a dark basement of a cruise bar with men in slings and the smell of cum and poppers. These longings were not my "disease" but rather my authentic desires.

I crave being social in the world in the company of my friends. I sometimes want to dance all night, shirt off, rubbing up against beautiful gay men, and ideally go back to bed with one or more of them. I crave fucking people I do not know who may or may not be consuming the substance of their own choosing, and I crave one-on-one sex with a well-known lover. As the booze and drugs became less and less important to me, drifting away into my past, I began to see that these cravings were not a part of some disease, but just Adam. These men, starting with Dan and Amine and then countless others, helped me to celebrate these desires rather than hide from them. These are my qualities, my strengths, and I will pray to no god to remove them from me.

Our strength cannot come from external validation. I needed to abandon counting days and accumulating an impressive statistic of sobriety in lieu of assessing the quality of my life and my interactions. Likewise, I cannot find power and strength in other typical forms of validation like landing (or losing) a client, achieving a benchmark in my work, or getting published. External praise is something I can strive for and be proud of so long as it does not indicate my value. Where I find value, where I find strength, now, is in the smiling eyes of a friend. It is found sitting quietly by the sea. It is lying in the arms of my partner, or him in mine. It is in sex and laughter and joy.

The seventh step told me to pray away my defects that led to my drinking; it gave me permission to not dig any deeper and not find my real reasons. I latched onto AA as I had to booze because I desperately needed a replacement mechanism to continue to hide from myself and my past. Those things are an unremovable part of me, and neither god nor AA can take them away.

I am not defective. I do not need a god to "remove" my supposed defects of character. I want to understand them, rename them, and heal from them where necessary. As clarity emerged on what I needed in order to heal, I could move forward. I could find that strength and power, and I could look more honestly at the actions of my past.

Only then would I be able to honestly assess where to seek forgiveness and how and to whom I actually needed to make amends.

8. Acknowledging those I have harmed, beginning with myself

I want to make right what I have done wrong, but to do so I must first forgive myself.

AA Step Eight: Made a list of all persons we had harmed, and became willing to make amends to them all.

I didn't really need to write an amends list. It was (and is) there in my head, a burning scroll of shame ever present inside of me. I drank so much because I felt (knew) that I was constantly failing and disappointing everyone in my life; so that list of people I had wronged took no effort to write. It took my sponsor several days to help me reduce it to those I had actually harmed. At the time, I was incapable of seeing that the greatest damage had been to myself.

I frequently recall what a woman in AA said to me after a meeting one day. I had shared something about searching for the turning point, the moment when I became this person who had lost control to alcohol. I could not find the exact time that my drinking had become a problem, and I was not yet able to see that the problem's source came into my life long before booze. She approached me after, as

131

we knew and liked each other, and I considered her to be intelligent, well-spoken, and kind.

"I was born with this disease," she announced. "Really?" I replied, a little shocked, "How do you know that?" She stated, "I just do. I have always been this way." I quickly found a reason to get away, overwhelmed by the feeling that what she was telling me was insane, but I did not know why. I replied, "I'm not sure I believe that," and excused myself.

Years later, in therapy, I found myself saying something similar, that I had been born broken. My therapist worked to help me undo that thinking, pointing out that a baby is not born with emotional baggage and damage, but rather learns those things in response to the actions of adults. He asked me, "Would you ever say that to anyone else, tell another person that they were just inherently, emotionally defective from birth?"

Now that I do not believe that we all drink excessively or abuse drugs because of some incurable birth defect or mysterious disease, but rather, use these chemicals to escape from our fear and pain, I can understand why her comment seemed so off to me. I now understand that we hurt ourselves, paradoxically, in an effort to stop the hurt. For most of us, the greatest harm has been inflicted by us upon ourselves.

It is a lovely idea, in step eight, to list the harms we have caused and be willing to make amends. It can be healing both for ourselves and for those we have caused pain, but it must start and end with the self. We all love some version of the saying, "If you can't love yourself, how can you expect anybody else to love you?" The same goes for forgiveness, for if I cannot see and forgive myself for the harm I have done to *me*, I will never believe or accept absolution from others. AA wanted me to list everyone else I had harmed, and so I did. It wasn't until after I had retreated from AA for some time that I realized the only name left on that list, written in invisible ink, was my own.

The idea that I was born damaged is a mask that I hide behind because it provides me with an excuse for what I believe is my inability to be better and to deserve love. It reinforces every fear within me, placing the healing from those fears outside my control. If this is "just how I am," then I preemptively give the world an excuse to not love me, because I am inherently unlovable. It absolves me from responsibility, takes all the onus off of those who damaged me, and neatly reiterates my self-loathing.

Every hangover, every drunken mistake, every night of excessive consumption was an act of harm against myself. In that place of damage, senses blurred and self-loathing elevated, I sometimes also did harm to others. It is an act of self-love to seek to change and repair damage done in my life, and it can start the process of healing, but it is unenduring unless I believe I also deserve that forgiveness.

Much of my pain comes from growing up in a world that openly hated queer people. But today, now, it is hard to remember or funny to think of that time before coming out. The distant experience of desperately wishing I were not gay can feel foreign and foolish to me now. Today, I love being queer and I would not change it for the world.

In my early teens I wanted so badly to be straight, but my hormones aggressively argued otherwise. I found myself masturbating thinking about my older brothers' friends, terrified I would get an erection in the locker room, and deeply in love with my own best friend. When his family drama exploded and he moved to Florida, I was devastated. I was also relieved because he was not like me, and I would never have to tell him or hear him say that he did not feel the same.

I clung to the idea of being bisexual because if I were bi it would mean I had a fifty-fifty chance to choose to be with a woman and keep my secret hidden. To this day I do not understand some gay men's disdain for bisexuality, for that tiny glimpse, even if false, of what it could be like to love and fuck any gender was something so beautiful that I wish it were true. Truth be told, the sex I had with women as a teenager and young adult was fantastic. I long to be pansexual, and I do wonder if my/society's fear and shame is blocking me still from that sexual potential.

Once I could no longer deny that I wanted to have sex with men, I clung desperately to the idea that I could not love another man. How could I know that I was simply reversing the psychology that the world had inflicted upon me? If I were gay, the world would despise me and want to inflict violence upon me. In hindsight it is so clear that I convinced myself I could not love men because I was taught that I would not be loved if I were to go down that path of sin, lust, and degradation.

By the time I got to college, I had kissed one boy (in a truth-or-dare game), and that was it. Sophomore year I let a man go down on me, but would not return the favor. Having had an orgasm, my head cleared and the terror set in, and I pushed him away. I got my own phone in my room so I could call phone-sex lines (remember those?!), but beyond that one experience I could not let myself engage sexually with men in real life, only the seemingly fictional, faceless voices coming through the phone. I finally broke up with my girlfriend, and when I had gotten myself good and drunk at the bars, I would come home and sleep with my gay (and very out) roommate. I still feel bad about how I drunkenly used his body at night, but rejected him in the daylight because I thought I could not allow myself to feel gay.

The summer after my junior year I stayed in my college town instead of going back to my small hometown, and I contemplated coming out. I had sex with one man, but in my confusion, I became obsessed with proving to him that it didn't mean anything to me. It ironically backfired, as he misinterpreted my insistence on being "cool" as wanting to be his boyfriend, and he stopped speaking to me. This left me more lost, rejected by a man I thought I didn't have feelings for, and yet my feelings were hurt. I didn't understand what I felt or who I was. I remember thinking, "I should just go back to being straight."

Then I met Ben. Early in my senior year, we had a drunken hook-up, but with Ben something was different. I would later see him in the halls of the theater department and get nervous. I did not really know him, but there had been a connection buried under the booze, more than anything I had let myself feel before. This boy, he knocked me over. His eyes made me jump, deep in my stomach, every time they caught my own.

By the time we ended up working together on a show later that year, I had (or so I thought) put that behind me. Then one day, we kissed. Then we fucked. We kept it a secret so the others on the show would not know, until the opening night party, when we kissed in front of everyone. To be honest, it was a highly sexual party and he was not the only person I was with that night, but when I kissed Ben it was different. I still remember my friend's voice cheering us on, as she had clearly known I was gay for some time (as did most people, I suspect). She saw the way I kissed Ben and it was like watching relief.

I fell madly in love with Ben. I could no longer pretend my sexual desires for men were just physical because I loved this man so much, more than I had thought I was capable of. He made me laugh from within my soul. When he said he loved me I knew it was true. When I woke up next to him, I was happier than I had ever been in my life before and possibly since.

He took me to Niagara Falls on a surprise trip. We explored each other's bodies and minds and navigated our similar fears of being queer together. When I graduated and he had another year of school, we did not try to possess each other or falsely maintain a long-distance relationship that two newly queer, barely adult men would not have been capable of. Even in our breaking up, we loved each other deeply and fearlessly, unselfishly setting each other free.

One night, I took Ben up to the hilltop country club where I had worked the summer before. I wanted to show him the view from there, something I had not shared with anyone. I had kept my love of its beauty even from my coworkers because I thought they would not understand, but I wanted Ben to see it. We sat on the hood of my car and the rain started to come down. With the radio playing and the lights twinkling, we had one of the most special moments of my whole life as our bodies became sopping wet with rain and sweat and tears and emotion.

Ben is still one of my dearest friends. This story does not, and will not, end in a straight version of a happy ending. For me, it is the happiest ongoing ending of all of the stories of my life. We have traveled together, we confide all of our truths to each other without reservation, and we have supported each other with love throughout all of the last two decades. Ben is my first love and I never fell out of love with him. He is my friend, my love, and he will be forever. I laugh until it hurts every time I speak with him.

Some people, usually straight, find that sad. I find it sad for them to not see how perfectly beautiful it is. With this man, I have experienced every version of love. Years ago, we held and made love to each other into an acceptance of who we both are today. We love each other beyond the bond of a label we had in 1998. Our souls are intertwined forever, and I have no doubt I will know him for the rest of our lives.

The rest of my coming out was certainly more challenging and less pleasant. I have been threatened and bashed and discarded and abused. I have also been loved and celebrated and cheered and held. That is life. But what I do have, what I will always have, is a shared experience where I learned I could love both men and myself, and I have Ben to thank for that.

Life is hard, and coming out does not fix that. But that magical moment of true, unabashed intimacy on the hood of a Honda more than twenty years ago, soaking wet and kissing the lips of the first man I ever loved, exists outside of the rest of my reality. That was just ours. That night solidified my ability to love and be loved by every man after, and I will never give that away. It was the moment I became truly queer, and it is the greatest gift I have ever received.

After Ben, my experiences were less than perfect. For reasons I am now beginning to understand, I subsequently chose men who were not like Ben. I found damaged men, usually with an alcohol and/or drug problem, who did not give me the love and compassion that Ben and I had shared. My drinking problem progressed with each of these men until I was mired in a non-stop cycle of drunk, ashamed, hungover, drunk again. In that spiral of regret and self-loathing, even the beautiful connections were shrouded in pain and a belief that I was inherently broken, tied to my alcohol abuse and therefore labeled as something I should be ashamed of.

Even so, I had the gift of loving Ben. I had proof that I could love and be loved. For many years I forgot that, or mutilated it, but I could not erase it entirely because this beautiful friend and love has always been in my life. When I was challenged to justify the belief that I had been born broken, the proof that I had not was there in Ben.

I have always sought out connections like the one I have with Ben. I did not need to make amends to the men I fucked and who fucked me. I did no harm to them, and I did nothing wrong by connecting and having consensual sex with other willing humans. The great harm in those often lovely experiences was that I twisted them, afterwards, into a weapon against myself. I needed sex and intimacy, and then I punished myself for seeking out bodies and touch because I felt I did not merit their contact. I was not terrible to these men. I was brutally harmful, the next day, to me.

I have certainly done harm to others and have made an effort to repair those damages where I am capable. I also make a concerted effort today to reduce the harm that I cause in the world. An honest assessment, post-AA, shows that I always wanted to be kind and good to others. Alcohol did not change that, and it did not make me selfish.

The greatest harm I did in my drinking and in my thinking was against my own self, and viciously so. I had to reverse the order that AA asked of me and put myself at the top of that list of amends. I needed to acknowledge that I was sometimes angry and hurt, and justifiably so, without having played any part in the harm done to me. Only in acknowledging and forgiving my self-harm could I cease trying to escape from or erase my past. Only after trying to forgive myself could I authentically accept the forgiveness of anyone else.

At the time, I was not yet able to do so, so I went out and made those amends to others. Today, I ask myself first, "Have I done any harm?" and "Did I do more harm to myself than others?" and even, sometimes, "Does this person deserve my forgiveness?" The answer to that last question is not always yes.

Sometimes, I am better off just letting someone go.

9. Seeking forgiveness without causing greater harm to myself

I seek forgiveness where I have done harm, including the lack of compassion for myself.

AA Step Nine: Made direct amends to such people wherever possible, except when to do so would injure them or others.

Everyone knows about making amends. We have all seen it in a multitude of films or on TV, and many of us have been on the receiving end of an amends in real life. I had, in my head, several very dramatic scenes of grand apology wherein I would tearfully express my deep shame and regret, and the recipient would be profoundly grateful, having waited so very long for my apology so our relationship could begin anew. They would also, of course, express their admiration for my recently adopted life choices. Sadly, or thankfully, this is not at all how it went.

My drinking had not significantly harmed my family as I do not live near any of my relatives. But being drunk every night and hungover every day did not make me the best son/brother/relative, as I rarely answered the phone or called back, particularly with my mom. My beautiful sponsor, here again, had such simple advice to make what he called living amends.

He told me simply that it might hurt my mother's feelings to tell her I had sometimes ignored her calls on purpose. Why not, he proposed, just start answering the phone?

I did make a few "I'm so sorry" type of amends to people whom I had directly harmed. One in particular was to a colleague. I had been hungover and impatient, and I had treated her horribly. I was deeply ashamed of my behavior. In the subsequent years, I ran into her frequently in professional contexts and we pretended not to know each other. To her, I sent an email expressing my regret at how I had spoken to her and admitting that my behavior had been in response to my own perceived failings, and not hers. I admitted in the letter that I had subsequently ignored her publicly because I was embarrassed at how I had treated her. I was too ashamed to look her in the eyes or speak to her.

She replied with a beautifully generous acceptance of my apology and a lovely expression that she looked forward to seeing me again without the unnecessary tension of events long in the past. That same night, impossibly, we ran into each other at a holiday party and shared a hug. To this day I still become emotional remembering her generosity of spirit, tearing up even as I write these words more than a decade later.

I did not mention to my colleague that I was sober, because my apology to her was warranted, deserved, and not part of some regimen for my own benefit. There was no before and after Adam. Active in my alcohol abuse, I sometimes lacked the patience and fortitude to conduct myself in a manner I could be proud of. I did not lack the desire to do so. Conversely, there were several times in those twelve sober years that I did not answer the phone or snapped at someone who didn't deserve it. Consuming alcohol or not, I felt bad for those times.

One of the changes in my thinking started when I realized the falseness of that story with my colleague. I incorporated that moment into my speaking at AA meetings, touting the beauty and power of step nine. Yet how it actually transpired was not part of my step work. I saw her one night at a show and saw that she avoided looking at me. I felt stupid and ashamed, so I wrote to her because our conflict had been of my making. Yes, I had been a drinker when the incident happened, but I felt terrible about it long before I got sober. I did not apologize as a way to further my sobriety. I apologized because, drinker or not, I felt bad about the way I had treated her. That is who I have always been.

Sexually, the list of men I had "harmed" was quite long. When my sponsor asked me repeatedly "What harm did you cause?" and when I could not say, the name was erased. In assessing harm, particularly for the sex-positive, we must challenge ourselves to see whose ethical scale we are applying to our lives. Shame is not the same as culpability, and feelings of guilt do not necessarily indicate damage done. So many of my not-needed amends helped me to, over time, separate my own morals from those imposed upon me.

I had done so much damage to myself by absorbing puritanical sexual ethics. I did not understand at the time, but I think my sponsor was trying to get me to forgive myself. I caused no harm to others when I had sex, but I still insisted on punishing myself the next morning and for years thereafter.

I needed to start answering the calls from my mother, but I also needed to start listening to my own heart and mind and body. Wanting an active and multi-partner sex life was not a product of my drunken immorality, yet I perceived a wrongdoing that did not exist. It did me a world of good to make amends to people I had wronged, and I am very grateful for that experience. I am still in the process of seeing, believing, and forgiving the harm I did to myself.

Other amends I thought I had to make were less straightforward. In AA, deeply ingrained in a mentality of finding "my part" in everything that had gone wrong, I minimized and eventually erased the violence and trauma of my childhood and the abuse of a relationship in my early twenties, but I would not admit that until later and with the help of that therapist. My "before" tale was one of a broken man of many faults and weaknesses who had succumbed to the power of the drink. I even thought I needed to make amends to that man who had physically, sexually, and emotionally abused me in young adulthood for having cut him out of my life.

In the rooms of AA, I would speak of parents that loved me (and still love me) unconditionally, but never of the violence in my childhood home. I would talk of my mother who always made sure to let me know I was loved, which was and continues to be true, but never of the impossible role of emotional support I became for her even before turning nine or ten years old. I would espouse that my family loves me, accepts me, and welcomed all of my boyfriends, but never speak of the years before coming out being called a fairy, a faggot, a queer, or of hearing unending Catholic rhetoric that I and my desires were sinful and repulsive. I would speak of my father as a good man, which he is, but I did not talk of the physical abuse and chaos he inflicted upon us in the early years.

147

I do not want this book to be a tale of blame. My parents are good and loving people who did their very best. Young and poor, alone in rural Maine, they were basically children themselves when they had me at ages twenty-two and twenty-five, and I was their third child. I love my parents deeply in spite of and even because of all they had to deal with. We are close today, and I have no desire to indict them. Today, they are there for me and their other children no matter what. I can call on them for anything at any time.

Because I do not want to hurt them, I also need to fight the desire to act as if I was not harmed. I used AA in the same way that I used substances, to eliminate, minimize, and forget my painful experiences. It is not AA's fault that I adjusted my narrative to fit its formula, but it is the inherent trap of that formula that sucked me in. I spoke eloquently of this young, loved man who descended into a life of drunkenness through no one's fault but his own and that of his disease, who then found redemption in the rooms of recovery, and I was rewarded.

The tears, the shining eyes, the nods, the hugs, and the gratitude I received when I changed my narrative to one of succumbing to then overcoming my disease of alcoholism prompted me to shift the blame entirely to my own mental, emotional, and spiritual malady. It also allowed me to continue avoiding the sources and origins of my pain. I never really examined why I drank so much. I could simply blame my disease.

As cliché as it sounds, the person I most needed to forgive was myself. The person who needs more compassion than I can give and the person I was cruelest to was me. I hold myself to standards and expectations I would never impose on anyone I love. In order to stop abusing alcohol (and to find sexual freedom without it) I needed to make amends to myself. Living, active amends, including reducing the hateful judgment with which I punish myself.

I eventually realized that in seeking the forgiveness of those who had, in fact, harmed me, I was doing incredible damage to myself. The narrative that I did not deserve the same love as others helped to reinforce this notion of "my part" in any resentment I had. Like any human, I have conflicts in my life that were my fault and conflicts caused by others. Making amends leaves no room for the latter, even though those events are often the cause of why we harm ourselves with substances.

I did not need AA to feel bad about the mistakes I have made in my life. I carry those with me always, dragging around a heavy sack of proof that I am a piece of shit. Had I continued with step nine in the recommended way, I would have done myself more harm than healing. I needed a different path.

I needed to step away from AA because I needed to stop myself from always finding "my part" and seeking the forgiveness of people who had done me harm, for I have finally learned that harm can go both ways. I needed to accept that I am a human who makes mistakes, but imperfection is not a defect. I needed to change the way I speak to and about myself, because if I continue to refer to myself with disgust, shame, anger, and impatience, I will inevitably want to harm that person again. As much work as I have done to understand and heal from my past, I am not free of that damage.

I am not a person who often does harm to others, but I struggle every day to be kind to myself.

10. Evaluating my present choices objectively and with compassion

I must remember, every day, that the shame-based morality of others has nothing to do with me.

AA Step Ten: Continued to take personal inventory and when we were wrong promptly admitted it.

In the early days of sobriety, the simplicity of the language in step ten, "and when we were wrong promptly admitted it," was very helpful. Trying to clarify my choices and see where I behaved in ways I felt ashamed of was easy to do by asking the simple question, "Was I right or wrong?" Like most analysis (particularly of oneself), things eventually get more complicated. Right and wrong are not simple universal standards. The question must eventually be asked, are those standards my own, or have they been imposed upon me?

Often in those gay AA meetings were examples of slut-shaming in the guise of step ten that I could not accept. I frequently heard the phrase "I acted out last night." These self-flagellating declarations were inevitably tied to sexual behavior and frequently to something benign and harmless like a one-night stand. I would sit there and listen to another fellow lament that he had gone on the apps and had anonymous sex and refer to this as old (bad) behavior. Nods of appreciation and support would round the rooms, encouraging us to leave behind those naughty inner sluts with a clear implication that if we did not, we could not remain sober. That was how drunk people acted.

I needed both qualifiers (have I done wrong *and* according to whom?) in order to clarify for myself what was and was not behavior I should regret. Certainly, in my past, while drinking excessively, I acted in ways that I should not have. I also acted in ways that my guilt, shame, internalized homophobia, and the insane standards I had set for myself would only allow under the influence of a substance.

As I began to explore my sexuality more and more, step ten further pushed me away from the program and into finding my own ethical scale. I do not want to lie, cheat, steal, or be aggressive or mean. I do not want to hurt people's feelings and I hope to live up to my word. These are daily inventories that I can assess with clarity. When I act terribly, I hate myself. When I hate myself, I want to punish or erase myself or, at the very least, my feelings. I know how to do that with substance abuse.

As I spoke at AA meetings, I often shared this cycle. Act badly. Feel shame. Get drunk. Wake up hungover and miserable. Act badly again. I would also speak of this cycle in sobriety, and how without doing an inventory of self, I could easily begin this cycle again. If I act in a way that causes me shame, I am more likely to feel the way I felt that drove me to abuse alcohol. Where it gets complicated is in deciphering the source of that shame.

If we continue to insist upon the existence of two selves, drunk and sober, then we continue, inevitably, to equate all "before" behavior with "bad" behavior. When I first went sober to sex clubs or participated in an orgy, I would feel that same old guilt and self-loathing. As I began to ask myself, speaking also with those few sober people who also lived out their happy, slutty lives, "Did I cause harm?" the truth quickly emerged: This shame was not my own.

There is value in pausing frequently to check in with oneself as this step suggests. Patterns of destructive behavior, often guided by fear-based self-righteousness, can quickly take hold of our lives. To frequently pause and honestly evaluate if one's own behavior is causing happiness or distress is to, hopefully, avoid establishing repetitious actions that cause one to hate oneself. It is a beautiful, useful tool.

It can also cause further repetitive harm. Most of us who abused substances are already prone to an exaggerated level of self-criticism caused by our fears, trauma, and deep inner unhappiness. We do not look kindly upon ourselves, the evidence of which is so clear in our pattern of self-destruction. Can we then do a daily evaluation without excessively labeling our actions as wrong and therefore ourselves as bad? When it comes to sex, with so much negative messaging around us, this becomes especially difficult.

Several times in therapy, my therapist would say something that surprised me. I would tell him some story of failure or shame, and he would look at me quizzically and say, "I'm not hearing what you did that was so bad." It usually made me laugh, having him point out my hyper-elevated tendency to self-criticize. One moment in particular stands out when I said, early on, "Am I allowed to tell you in detail about sex stuff?" He just laughed out loud. "Yeah, Adam," he said, "you can talk about sex stuff in therapy."

He helped me to see that I needed to discern whose voice was guiding my judgments. When I woke up ashamed of a sexual escapade, if I asked myself if I had done harm to my partner(s) or to myself, the answer was always that I had not. In those instances,

I began to see that my negative feelings about my sexuality were not based on the damage I had done, but in the external judgments I was easily susceptible to.

Several years ago, I found myself in a cruising bar, sober, in southern Spain. I looked across the crowded room of naked and mostly naked bodies to see a pair of beautiful eyes locked with mine. He smiled. There was a man on his knees in front of him, but the moment was ours. Between we two.

I crossed the room. Touched his chest. He touched mine. Our faces moved slowly together, and I traced his jawline with my finger as a man on the other side of the room screamed in ecstasy/agony. His lips grazed mine and we kissed, softly. Then passionately. Then deeply, and hard, and long, and I felt him moan inside my mouth as the man before him became more excited by our kissing and took him deeper into his mouth.

For what seemed like hours, we kissed and touched, laughed and bit, smiled and moaned and pinched and licked each other until finally his body shuddered with orgasm and his face fell into my neck. He breathed hotly on my body, then finally pulled his face up to mine. He kissed me again, slow and long and intimate. I had forgotten where we were.

He thanked the man who was still on his knees and grabbed my hand, pulling me toward the other room, the bar. He wanted to talk. He stopped three times on the short journey from one room to the other to kiss me again.

His English was almost as broken as my Spanish, so we laughed and fumbled our way through the basics, occasionally grabbing a nearby stranger or the bartender to see if they could translate a word or phrase. Throughout, I touched him, kissed him, held him, and ran my hands over and over his body, and he did the same to me. He was funny, sweet, and his eyes were shockingly kind. They flashed with a spark of light every time we leapt over a linguistic hurdle and landed on another moment of understanding of one another.

I have since become friends with this man and our connection is not romantic. There were times I have felt that he wished that our initial connection had turned into coupling. I have had to fight the urge to feel bad about this and perceive that I had done something wrong and caused him some harm. The moment I shared with him was honest and real, and my feelings that were more amicable than romantic in subsequent weeks were also true.

Even so, I can twist that moment using this thinking of having always caused harm and needing to "promptly admit it." He has never asked me to feel guilt or shame. Our ongoing friendship is proof that I caused him no harm. When I reject this mentality, taking a step back from my automatic instincts to see myself negatively, I can see that both the moment we shared and the friendship we now have are positive. No amends need to be made.

I find myself fighting these deeply ingrained instincts almost daily. A conflict at work, a rough week for a friend, having great sex when I know my boyfriend has not gone out in a while, and many other examples of things that are not wrongdoing will still send me spiraling into shame. I have to untangle these things in order to actually see if I am responsible for the things that go wrong in the lives of others. Most often, I am not. I do not control the happiness of those I love or have any power over the shit that happens in our world.

There is an odd irony in the enormous ego of self-loathing. I see myself as small and unlovable and I see myself as responsible for everyone around me. I cannot have it both ways. It is often a relief to deflate that ego and realize that not only is it not my job to fix him, it, or you, but also that I am incapable of doing so. It now makes me laugh and helps me to breathe when I can see that, in fact, there is nothing I can do to fix things. Just being there for a friend is enough.

Life, the internet, idioms, my past, religion, politics, and nearly everything else can make me adopt the moral compass of others. America's obsession with work and success, which I believe in less and less, can make me feel terrible for taking a much-needed bit of time off. Society's disdain for fetish and multi-partner sex will still creep in, causing me to feel shame the morning after a wonderfully sexual evening with multiple strangers. None of this is my own.

In sex, I find myself most often at odds with the morality of others. I love sex. Sex is awesome. It makes me and my partners feel good, seen, attractive, and relieved. We pleasure one another and that is a good thing. That is positive. That is joyous. That is not wrong. When I indulged in and shared that beautiful moment with a man I later did not pursue a romance with, that was not wrong.

I have no reason to feel shame or embarrassment for having brought joy to myself and others. In fact, I should be celebrating the freedom and opportunity to do so. I can fuck whomever I choose, and because those people are always consenting adults, I have no reason to feel shame, even if it resembles something I used to do when drunk. My only part in any shame I feel about that is I am still carrying around the bullshit that others have heaped upon me.

It is difficult to shake off those ideas. It is not easy to remember that my journey toward healing is ongoing and that I will never completely eradicate the dark voices of my past and my shame. I have to be careful when I assess what and to whom I have done wrong.

To do so I must return, regularly, to that light within me that wants what is best for me.

11. Engaging actively with my sources of strength and healing

To heal, to grow, and to love, I need to embrace and celebrate every version of light, joy, sensuality, and freedom that pushes out my shame and teaches me to love myself.

AA Step Eleven: Sought through prayer and meditation to improve our conscious contact with God as we understood Him, praying only for knowledge of His will for us and the power to carry that out.

Prayer is not for everyone. I love meditation, but it is not a practice that is helpful to all, and many find it frustrating. Some believe in a god of some kind; others do not. Many, myself included, just do not know. Yet, somehow, we have to learn to continuously reconnect to an energy, whatever it is, that drives us to make choices toward a healthier life. Something within each of us, however small, wants us to not hurt ourselves or others. That source, that light, that voice, whatever it may be, is where I can return to guide my choices.

The antithesis of that source is fear and shame. I am afraid that you will see me and you will find me not worthy. I am ashamed of both my anger and my weakness and I want neither of these to see the light of day. These elements, inside of me and all of us, lead me to hide, to retreat, and to hurt myself. I must learn to listen to the voice that wants me to heal rather than the verbiage of my fear, but these two voices often sound very much the same.

The literature of AA was written in the 1930s by white, straight, cis, Christian men. There are many things written in that book (and subsequent supporting texts) that are helpful. Particularly in *Twelve Steps and Twelve Traditions* there are implications or even direct statements that eventually you will abandon your foolishness and accept god (Christ) into your life. These do not help. In the eleventh step, the writers assume that you have, by now, found god or are just clinging to your foolishness: "We well remember how something deep inside us kept rebelling against the idea of bowing before any God."

That language of "His will for us" does not work for me. I do not know if god exists or what it even means if there is a god. I could not find the strength to avoid substance abuse through something so external, ethereal, and possibly false. Additionally, I find it hard to believe that even if such an all-knowing deity exists that it would care what happens to me, let alone have a specific will for my life. There are wars, destruction, global warming, poverty, starvation, violence, and countless other horrible things happening all the time. If there's a god up there, she's busy.

In my experience, the existence of and a relationship with a god is not the least bit necessary for one to want to heal. The challenge is that so many of us began to abuse drugs or alcohol because our past, frequently our childhoods, taught us to doubt our own worth. A god won't change that; my past is my past.

The key for me in the present is to locate a source of love. Sometimes that source of good and light, of love, is within me. I can meditate and find that inner force wherein resides the desire for me to grow and shine. It wants me to love myself and to love others. It is kindness and compassion, and it wants serenity. It wants joy. After a time, I found that it also wants sex.

Sometimes I need to look elsewhere because the other inner voice, the fear and the doubt and the shame, speaks louder than the part of me that loves myself. In these times, I must look without and find other sources of healing energy. There are times the sea works for me; there are times that rituals and spiritual practices work for me. I can also look to the love of my chosen family, my lovers, my blood family, and my friends—anyone who truly wants to see me in less pain. It is easiest to find in the laughter of someone I care for.

For a time, I found that love in the practice of my sobriety and in the rooms of AA, but at a certain point, sobriety was no longer enough. AA was no longer enough. The love of those around me could not provide me enough strength to continue this process of healing and self-care because I had not addressed the source of the pain within myself.

The program taught me to live a life without alcohol, and I usually believe that I needed that freedom, that clarity of thought and lack of destruction, to render myself capable of the next step. That next step did not exist for me in the rooms or texts of Alcoholics Anonymous. The next step was to walk away. There is no blame in that, except in that I found many people who insisted that the entire solution was there in the program and that leaving would inevitably lead to my self-destruction.

I cannot tell you the number of times I was told that if I walked away from AA, I would come "crawling back." I understand that fear, but I do not agree with hurling your fear at others. Perhaps for some, AA was the only safe haven where they could avoid returning to a life of peril and self-harm. For me, it was not. I needed to walk away to fully live my life. I imagine some of those people will say this book is proof that I am heading down the wrong path. I have had several experiences that lead me to believe the opposite.

The first time I ever found myself in a sling was in a sex club in Madrid. That aforementioned sober boyfriend, Amine, and I went on vacation, and we were well into our sexual exploration. We were at the point where we could go to a sex club together without any rules. You have your fun, I will have mine. If that means we are having fun together, great, and if not, great. The only rule was that we went home together at the end of the night, and it worked for us.

There was a tall, sexy, Spanish man that I had been making eyes with all night. We had seen each other at the bar a few times and caught each other's gaze more than once when one or the other of us was engaged with another man. Finally, as the night waned, I found myself in front of him with a sling directly behind me. He grabbed me, and we kissed. Hard, then intimate, then hard again. Our hands discovered every inch of each other's bodies, and we moved seamlessly between biting and caressing, aggressive and gentle, intimate and carnal. With my clear physical consent, he became a bit more aggressive.

He pushed me into the sling and entered me so fast I screamed. He paused, slightly, to be sure it was pain and pleasure and not just the former, but I told him with my eyes he should keep going. He did, taking me with a force I had never experienced. Suspended in a sling for the first time, I did not need to worry about balance or position. I did not have to figure out where to put any part of my body. I was cradled in the leather and held aloft by chains, and he took me, and I let go of control as he ravished me.

Later, as we walked to the bar, chatting, I introduced him to my boyfriend. "Congrats," said Amine, "I have never heard him scream like that." We all laughed. There was no shame. No jealousy. No embarrassment that this man had torn through my body and my inhibitions, and I had succumbed to every bit of it. There was only joy.

The three of us walked home, nearing dawn, and talked about Spain and travel and culture. His English was much better than my Spanish, and we were able to talk non-stop until we reached the intersection where we needed to part ways. "Want to get lunch tomorrow?" he asked me. "I would love to." I replied, and we exchanged numbers. I went home with my boyfriend and we fell asleep in each other's arms.

Lunch was lovely and that man is still my friend. He helped me get tickets to a few events years later when I found myself in Madrid again. I have met his very sexy husband. We have given each other advice and guidance via social media over the years, but mostly we just exchange witty comments or a laugh.

If I'd had this experience earlier in my life, it would not have been the same. I would have woken up ashamed and foggy and probably not have met him for lunch. Earlier boyfriends would have gotten jealous and imposed some other meaning on the interaction. I remembered every detail, and because I could not deny I had consciously made my choices, I held no shame about what I had done. I still chuckle a bit thinking about how loud I must have been for Amine to have heard me from the bar.

I tell this story because I find it beautiful. Without chemicals railing through my system, I was able to be both animalistic and sensual. I was able to be taken aggressively by this man and still see him as a lovely human I wanted to share a meal with. I did not shy away from him afterwards, nor did I feel like I needed to hide anything from my then-boyfriend. Ironically, ignoring the advice I heard in the rooms and becoming a raging slut while still sober taught me all of my greatest lessons about intimacy. The first, the most important, is that it is possible under almost any circumstances to be wildly primal and humanistically connected at exactly the same time.

It was also one of my versions of prayer and meditation. Suspended in mid-air, giving over control to another, and letting the absolute joy wash over my body, was religious. That was a connection to my higher power. It was self-love and self-care and came from a desire for me to heal from my shame and bask in the joy of getting beautifully, deeply penetrated.

There is, of course, an intrinsic connection between the rampant drug and alcohol abuse in the gay community and our deeply ingrained fear of intimacy. The problem is exacerbated in American culture, where the notions of maleness are so deeply rooted in a fucked-up combination of capitalism and misogyny that we perceive intimacy, emotion, and openness as weakness. Sex is conquest until it is coupled; then and only then can we call it love.

For young gay men, having absorbed all of these notions of sexuality, we must then attempt to process this information through a lens of homophobia, coming out, and the disappointment of our families and communities as a result of our sexual orientation. Even for those of us with eventually supportive families, there is no erasing that initial wish that it were not so, that we were not queer. That experience in the months or years leading up to our coming out lives within us into adulthood.

Given that we've been lambasted over our entire childhoods by the combined message that sex is dirty and gay sex is worse, it's no surprise that many gay men may need chemical substances to quell the fear and engage in sex. We need a few drinks to lubricate our courage and silence the voices of our shame. As such, intimacy can be the last thing on our minds as we begin to actively explore our sexuality, and any possible emotional connections are diminished further by a chemically created barrier. The non-intimate nature of our sexual interactions can be then reinforced by the emotional absence of our partners. American men in particular lead with apathy and coolness in order to avoid the appearance of vulnerability, and a pattern is established. The drugs and alcohol enhance that false fearlessness and allow us to engage in sex without indulging our emotions, or at least pretending not to do so.

Whether or not one has had a substance abuse problem, these fears exist. We have all absorbed the shame and anger of those that believe only a coupled, monogamous life is valid. We are all products of our environment and of a society that does not support open, communicative, and free sexual exploration. Any American who has had the desire to expand their sexual repertoire has battled these oppositions and a profound lack of understanding and support from our peers.

These problems are not unique to AA, but they are exacerbated there. So many who come into the rooms have done as I did, allowing this deeply ingrained sexual shame to find its relief in sobriety. We did not fuck like we used to fuck when we were broken, drunk, and high, so the equation of these behaviors is all too easy to make—but it is false. I craved the bodies and fluids and intimacy of others, and I let myself indulge those desires when I was drunk. The cause and effect I learned in AA are in the reverse order. I did not fuck because I was drunk. I got drunk so I could fuck. So I could connect.

The separation I needed to make from AA in order to celebrate my sexuality was the catalyst that led me to the next step of growth in therapy. I was still not drinking, I was out in the world and discovering love, intimacy, sex, fetish, community, self-expression, and yet I still felt lost. I had come to realize the answer to my problems was not in drunkenness, but I was becoming more and more sure that AA had reached the limits of its potential to help me. I needed more help, different guidance, and new ideas to look within myself and continue the process of healing.

The unexpected, somewhat paradoxical gift of therapy was finding that I needed not only to look toward the sources of light and goodness to take the next steps of my growth. I needed to also return to my pain and the violence and unintended damage of my childhood. I needed professional guidance to do so safely. I needed realize and admit out loud that I am always afraid.

AA cannot and should not guide us on this journey. The problem is that it tries to. The program insists that we stay involved and active forever. It diagnoses us with a chronic disease and teaches us to let that be the end of the exploration. Members of AA often insist that there is no graduation, but should there not be? If healing is the caring education of the self, do we not need to move on to the next level in order to continue learning?

Therapy is not religion. I did not find god on the proverbial couch. I found professional guidance; I found the space to say aloud things I had hidden for three or four decades; and I found out that I speak to myself in hateful ways with language that I would never, ever use on anybody else I care for. My therapist is not a priest or a higher power, but he is a teacher who helped me unveil my past pain and finally, slowly begin to heal. He is but one of the many connections between myself and the source of my healing.

To connect to my version of "god's will" (a life in which I do not harm myself) I needed to understand how, when, and why I stopped loving myself. No god or disease took my love of self away from me, and it cannot give back something it does not possess. I realized that the voice of compassion for myself was no longer speaking, but sobriety was not enough to embark on the journey of finding it and listening to it again.

That voice first came back to me through sex. It was there in that sling in Madrid. Before these sexual explorations, the sex-negative messaging of the world so resembled the Adam-negative messaging inside my own head. As I began to shut out those external sources of shame and celebrate my sexuality with the bodies of many, many men and in many spaces AA told me I should not and could not go, I found a way to start to love myself.

That is finding my higher power. There are days I am so angry at our society that shames people away from getting in touch with joy and ecstasy as a form of healing and light. It took me so long; I wasted so much time before I could accept that sex was not me doing something dark and wrong. Sex is the same as laughter, foolishness with friends, and cuddling. Sex is connecting to that part of you that wants you to be happy and sharing that with others.

We can help each other to take one step at a time toward constructing a sexual identity that does not involve annihilating ourselves with chemicals or drowning ourselves in shame. It is possible to start wandering the pathways of our sexual desire with small, safer experiments in order to discover for ourselves what we want. Trust me, there is power in this experimentation, and you may find that your sexuality is vaster than you currently imagine.

Wherever you can find that hope, that healing power, I encourage you to go to that space, and if that power is in the basement of a cruising bar, allowing yourself to be touched by the hands, mouths, and cocks of strangers so you feel beautiful and alive, so be it. Do not let anyone tell you what beautiful looks like to you. Decide that for yourself.

I, too, am damaged, fractured, and constantly in need of help, and the sources of that help can be as varied as my own past. I try to not reject that compassion and light from whatever beautiful, complicated, non-traditional place from which it might arrive. I also know that each person's experience is unique. We are not all the same. I have no idea how you can heal, and no amount of healing on my side can equip me to tell you what to do on yours.

So why am I telling you my story?

12. Sharing what has helped me without knowing what is best for you

I believe in the power and beauty of sharing stories, so I will tell you mine, but without implying that I know what your story should be.

AA Step Twelve: Having had a spiritual awakening as the result of these Steps, we tried to carry this message to alcoholics, and to practice these principles in all our affairs.

Step twelve is where I hit the biggest stumbling block of incongruity between my personal morality and the program of AA. We are told in this step to "practice these principles in all of our affairs." The principles I was being taught, or at least the ethical messaging I was receiving in the meetings, was frequently delivered under the rhetoric of "sober thinking" and "sober behavior." All too often, this meant a life of conformity in which sexual adventurism and individualism were rejected as the lifestyle of non-sober people. It also meant accepting your incurable disease.

How could I practice these supposed principles and remain true to myself?

I do not believe an active, promiscuous sex life is that of a powerless person, nor is it an insanity that needs correction. How could I turn my will over to a group whose ethics I did not believe in? My moral inventory did not match their morals, and I often found I could not share without being shamed. My sexual desires and my complicated past are neither defects of character nor shortcomings I wish for any god to remove. Consensual, adult sex is beautiful, not harmful, and the amends I needed to make were often to myself for absorbing the guilt and shame of others. In my personal inventory, I do not find a moral failing in having frequent, multiple sexual partners; I do not find that behavior to be wrong. If there is a god, and they want me to stop having sex, I will not pray to such a god.

I journeyed through these steps, and while each brought something into my life, I progressively found myself retreating from AA. The process was slow and long, but as I became more and more used to a life free from substance abuse, I also found that the morality, the principles, of the group that helped me applied only to certain and very limited parts of my life. Not in all of my affairs.

I came into AA for one reason: to stop abusing alcohol. With the help of AA, I stopped, but to then adhere these same tools to everything else seemed not only to be inapplicable, but arrogant. One book written by straight dudes in the 1930s cannot contain all or even most of the answers. It simply does not have any guiding principles for a sex-positive queer life in the following century.

As for carrying the message, I cannot. I am not sober and do not believe in most of the message. Well before I began drinking again, I found myself in conflict with this step. I will happily share my story with anyone who asks to hear it. I will offer support and love to anyone who tells me they are struggling and who wants to find a solution to their drinking or drug problem. I was given so much love, guidance, and kindness in the process of changing my drinking; I do agree it is my obligation to pass on that help, and I happily do so.

I also know that I do not have the answers. I do not know how anyone else should live. I do not have any idea when is the right time or what is the right method for you to address your substance abuse issues, because only you can decide that. If you ask me, I will share. If you need me, I will show up. If you do not want my help, it is none of my business what you do with your life and your choices. I cannot say that I know any better than another person, so I will not impose what I thought was best for me upon you.

There was a time, soon after quitting drinking, when I wanted to go out in the world and teach everybody what I had learned. At the same time, I was becoming resentful of sober gay men telling me how I should live my life. The paradox of these two feelings taught me a great lesson: I should never impose my morals or choices on anybody else.

I do not know that my ideas will work for you, and I do know that over time they will change and evolve. As such, I have no right to tell you how I think you should live. Even this book is hopefully nothing more than an explanation of my journey, but I am not so arrogant as to think it should become any version of a guideline for your own.

I try to tell my tale only with the understanding that my path is my own, neither the only nor the best, but simply the one that I took. If something in my story can help you to understand your own, that is a beautiful gift to us both. If not, I only wish for everyone to find their own way, enduring the least amount of pain possible. My true hope is only that you are inspired to heal, and that has nothing to do with following any path I chose to take.

I no longer believe that total abstinence is the only or even the best way to address a problem with drugs or alcohol, so I cannot share my tale with the hope that you will follow in my chosen footsteps. With a sexual life that deconstructed many so-called truths, and with a therapist shepherding me through trauma I previously denied, I have come to learn that the cause of my drinking was not an incurable disease. At the time, total abstinence from alcohol was the only option I knew, so that is the one I chose.

I do, however, wonder if that choice delayed for far too long my ability or willingness to look at the pain of my past. I turned AA into my drug, consuming it with vehemence, until one day I realized I was creating new, program-based narratives to replace the old, drunken ones, and neither story told the truth. Now, today, I talk these things through with a qualified therapist and caring friends, sometimes over a glass of wine.

If a person asks me how I stopped harming myself with booze, I will tell them. Of course, I hope that something in my words might trigger something in that person to help them to start their own journey toward self-harm reduction. We all like to be helpful, but I do not expect or even advise anyone to follow my path. There is a chance my story might be a small piece of what propels you toward a better life, and for that reason, I share it.

The same goes for sex. I do not want everyone to become a proud slut. I do not think everyone should join me in the basement of my favorite cruising bar and experiment with piss, bondage, and pain. I also do not think everyone should be monogamous. I think everyone should choose whatever works for them, with the right to change their mind, and be celebrated for that choice.

There are countless options, lifestyles, fetishes, and sexual explorations, and each person has the right to see what turns them on without being shamed or punished and the right to try something else, at any point. I will share my sexual stories with you, too, if you ask. Or for that you can just read this book, I suppose. Though there are many more stories …

Either way, the choice is yours and that is gorgeous. If I can be useful in your desire to heal and undo your shame and fear, I am happy to. I do not carry any great message. I rely on others all the time to help me, as my journey is ongoing and the pain and shame of my past are far from gone. I cannot fix you, nor do I want to, because you are not broken, and neither am I.

We are all doing our best, and sharing our journeys can be beautiful so long as we respect and remember that everyone has the right to their own choices, no matter what we might think another should do.

AFTERWARD

Programs of recovery exist to help the participant stop abusing drugs and/or alcohol. For that, they are beautiful and necessary, and I am very much in support of their continued existence. What they do not do, cannot do, is address the original source. I may or may not have needed to stop drinking to clear my life and my head enough to begin to heal. I stayed in that cycle for many years, healing only from the immediate, negative effects of drunkenness and hangovers, but not from the pain, shame, and confusion that caused me to drink in the first place.

I cannot say enough that it is vital that one seeks help from sources qualified to help. I heard many times in AA meetings that the twelve steps could be applied to any problem, and that is, in my experience, not true. In defense of the program, they do encourage outside help (therapists, doctors, etc.), but there is an underlying sense that those things should be secondary. "Sobriety comes first" we are told, over and over again. At first, maybe, that was true. In the long term, I disagree. My life, my healing, my exploration of why I had become this raging drunk need to supersede those personal journeys that address only the present.

I needed a therapist, not an unqualified fellow or a 100-year-old book, to shine the light on my lies or I would have circled that same drain, sober, but endlessly. I believed so strongly in the twelve steps because so much immediate pain had been relieved. I was not drunk every night, hungover every morning, or so desperately, frighteningly alone dealing with my shame. That relief was enormous, so I heaped upon AA a level of power it does not possess. I also used that false strength to avoid, as I had done with booze, looking deep within myself and asking why.

Being a slut was the catalyst to my eventual healing. As I explored my sexuality, fetish, and fantasies in spaces and situations that my sober fellows had adamantly insisted I avoid, I unconsciously started to withdraw from the program. I was still attending meetings and in touch with my sponsor, but I found myself speaking much less at the front of the room and raising my hand to share less and less often from the back. This slight retreat, plus the opening up of my sexual experience, gave me enough space to realize that something, even after several years sober, was still very wrong.

Sexually free and having broken down some of the falsehoods in my own story, I could finally look at the reasons why I had been such a drunk for so long.

AA teaches that alcohol and drug abuse is an inevitable response to an inherent, possibly genetic disease. I have no idea if that is true for others, but it is not universally true. It is not my truth.

My reasons for drinking began during my childhood and were exacerbated by homophobia, the AIDS crisis, an abusive relationship, and other losses and failures that all fit neatly into my perception of myself as unlovable and unworthy. As an adult, with help, I could finally start to heal.

From that first threesome to that sling to that man who pissed on me to the sheer number of men I've enjoyed, I've made beautiful, sex-positive connections with men who did not care if I drank or not. These men always prioritized my consent and safety. The shame reduced. I became more open and honest about my sexuality, with very few negative consequences. The filth and intimacy alike opened a space inside of me to see that I was desired. The myth that I was unlovable unraveled. I began to believe that I could be loved.

My sexual liberation handed me the keys to unlock the pain of my past, so when I walked into that therapist's office, I was so very ready to finally take the power away from that hurt and begin the process of healing. My sluttiness showed me that some of my shame was only hurting me from within; this revelation allowed me the space and breath to look at the rest. I am still fighting to regain my own power, but it was sex that opened the first door and let in a bit of light. Over the past years I have slowly, one tiny step at a time, been on a journey back to myself. My substance abuse was nothing more than a liquified attempt to drown that self whom I despised and whom I deemed unworthy of love.

I want to live. I want to love. I want to laugh. I want to fuck. I want to experience things unknown, and I want the freedom to do so without guilt or aggression. I want you to come with me if you desire to do so, and I want to not judge you for your choices that are so very different from my own. I want to allow the fluidity of sexuality, intellect, and emotion to exist at each stage of my life without negative dismissal of my past experience or closed doors to the future possibilities.

How is doing so not healthy and beautiful?

Can we not let each person examine their sexual desires under the clarity of a substance-free mind and unlearn and relearn what it means to be queer, sexual, and active? Can recovery not include a process of helping each other discern between our true desires and those that are self-destructive? Can recovery not include different paths for different people? Why do we think one diagnosis and one treatment is universally best for all cases? It is not. There are many others out there, so why do we only propose the one?

Piece by piece, and with compassion for the self, we can explore our own minds and fantasies and decide which acts are the result of authentic desire. Sometimes it is not so clear, the dichotomy of our damage and our shame playing out in complicated ways. We can re-try these things, without chemical enhancement, and decide for ourselves what is for me, what is not, and what might be something to try later as I move in the direction of sexual liberation. We can also learn, grow, and change our minds.

I have been damaged by a world that hated me, and I can walk into a cruise bar, a bathhouse, or a relationship armed with the choice of how I will respond to that damage and how I will celebrate my survival. When I am sexually submissive, I can both relive my pain and enact my power to choose my own experience and have an orgasm as a result of that act. Or sometimes not. Sometimes it just feels really fucking good to relinquish control, and I love it. When I am dominant, pounding myself into a submissive bottom in front of other men, I am both celebrating my power and respecting and loving (yes,

I mean love) that man who is taking control of his own past. Or maybe he isn't. Maybe he just really likes getting fucked in front of an audience. And when I love another man, I am both chasing my trauma and deeply exposing myself to another, worthy human. All of these are true, interconnected, and simultaneous.

The experience of hitting rock bottom is terrifying, painful, and demoralizing. Every story is different but a frequent common denominator in many is the feeling of being lost, broken, and helpless. Hopefully, with love and support, one can begin to rebuild. One can stand up and reconstruct a new, healthier life toward an ideal or ideals that had been abandoned to the abuse of drugs or alcohol. Each new life, each set of goals, each shining possibility of a future self is unique and stunningly beautiful, and each should be celebrated.

At that point, we have the glorious gift of choice. You may not want the life and self I wish to build and celebrate, and I will not want yours. I only ask that you allow me and others the freedom and give me the love to create my own free self, and I will try to do the same for you. In that, there is no shame, there is less fear, and the possibility that true recovery, in whatever form that takes, whether from substance or self, might be realized.

ACKNOWLEDGMENTS

First and foremost, I need to thank Alex Brousset. His guidance, his patience, and his ability to help me veer toward my own ideas (and away from those imposed upon me) is one of the main reasons I was able to write this book. I want to thank my family, for even when we make mistakes, we also make sure to tell each other, "I love you." That love has always been a force in my life and is a beautiful gift. My family has always encouraged me to follow my own path, and they are here with me on this new journey as a writer. I want to say a huge thank you to Steven Strafford, James Patrick Benn, and Lindsey Murray for taking the time to read the early, clunky drafts of this book and giving me advice and feedback that shaped it into what it is today. I am so lucky to have intelligent, honest friends who will both celebrate me and gently tell me when I am off track. They also constantly encourage me, making me feel like I need to, and can, continue. Thank you from the bottom of my heart to all of my exes, for without you I would be a very different person. Because of you all, I know so many versions of love. Perhaps most importantly, I need to thank Ellen Vessels, this book's incredible editor. Without their guidance and intelligence, ranging from meticulous proofreading to astoundingly insightful commentary, this text would be a much longer, much messier, version of itself.

Thank you to Domenic Mykel for the introduction to Ellen. Merci à Denis Trauchessec for your beautiful cover design. Thank you to all of the queer and honest writers I've read in the past few years who have inspired me to tell my truth. The bravery of queer writers and your honest, searing work are what got me through these final edits. Last, but far from least, I need to send out a huge thank you to all of my sexual partners over the years. The experiences we had helped me to see the world through a different, more open, and loving lens that did not exist before we shared our selves and our bodies with each other.

Printed in the USA
CPSIA information can be obtained
at www.ICGtesting.com
LVHW021523131023
760849LV00042B/109